GIFT GIVEN: COACH CURT BICKLEY

DATE: AUGUST 2015

GREEN BAY REPLAY

GREEN BAY REPLAY

The Packers' Return to Glory

DICK SCHAAP

AVON BOOKS ◆ NEW YORK

AVON BOOKS
A division of
The Hearst Corporation
1350 Avenue of the Americas
New York, New York 10019

Copyright © 1997 Dick Schaap
Interior design by Kellan Peck
Insert photographs by Dan Kramer
Visit our website at **http://AvonBooks.com**
ISBN: 0-380-97595-5

Library of Congress Cataloging in Publication Data:

Schaap, Dick, 1934–
    Green Bay replay : the Packers' return to glory / Dick Schaap.
        p. cm.
    1. Green Bay Packers (Football team)—History.   2. Super Bowl (Football
game) I. Title.
GV956.G7S4   1997   97-23015
                                                                      CIP

First Avon Books Printing: September 1997

AVON TRADEMARK REG. U.S. PAT. OFF. AND IN OTHER COUNTRIES, MARCA REGIS-
TRADA, HECHO EN U.S.A.

Printed in the U.S.A.

FIRST EDITION

QPM   10 9 8 7 6 5 4 3 2 1

16-0 S82G

This one is for my own Pack, my starting eleven:
My six children,
Renée, Michelle, Jeremy, Joanna Rose, Kari, and David;
and my five grandchildren,
Noah, Joshua, Benjamin, Elana, and Daniel.

Contents

GREEN BAY REPLAY

Introduction

My son Jeremy arrived in New Orleans the afternoon before the Super Bowl, picked up his date, and led her to Bourbon Street in the French Quarter. They pushed their way through a sea of green and gold, wall-to-wall Green Bay Packer fans, jamming the street, spilling out of the bars, waving from the balconies. Jeremy and his date made slow progress, finally coming to a halt, their path blocked by a thick cluster of Packer fans, crowded around someone unseen, clamoring for autographs and photographs. "What's going on?" the young woman asked Jeremy. "Who is it?"

Jeremy stood on his tiptoes, found a line of vision to the center of the pack. He shook his head, bemused, and smiled. "Who is it?" his date asked again.

"It's my father," Jeremy said.

They asked me to sign cocktail napkins, T-shirts, hats, footballs, chests, even one navel. They asked me to pose with wives, girlfriends, boyfriends, and children. They thanked me for the books and articles I had written about the Green Bay Packers, and for the kind words I had spoken on television and radio about their team. They crushed me with affection.

Never in almost half a century of covering sports had I enjoyed such attention. I felt almost like a Packer.

Obviously, I do not come to this book with clean journalistic hands. I am not objective. Not about Green Bay, the town or the team, the fans or the football players. I am emotionally involved. I love the men who coached and played for the Green Bay Packers in the 1960s. I like the men who coach and play for the Green Bay Packers in the 1990s. Every time I think of the city and the people who live there, I smile.

I visited Green Bay for the first time in 1961, when I was in my twenties, when Vince Lombardi was on the brink of his first National Football League championship, and in the years that followed, the coach and his family, his wife Marie and his brother Joe and his son Vince, and the men who played for him became my acquaintances and then my friends.

Jerry Kramer, the right guard, became my closest friend. We worked together on four books, and by the fourth, *Distant Replay*, our account of a reunion of the team that won the first Super Bowl, we knew each other so well we could communicate almost without words, with little more than a glance or a nod. We commiserated during our divorces and celebrated our remarriages, and marveled that we helped to raise six children apiece. Jerry is the godfather of Jeremy, my older son. Jerry's son Dan lived with me and my family while he apprenticed as a newspaper photographer at New York *Newsday*.

Fuzzy Thurston, the left guard, is my permanent host in Green Bay. He owns a neighborhood saloon called Shenanigans, a shrine to Packers past and present, and whenever I land at Austin Straubel Airport, my rented car, as if it had a mind of its own, pulls away from the terminal, veers right onto highway 172, crosses over the Fox River, then circles back onto South Monroe Avenue, heading, almost automatically, for Shenanigans. Invariably, Fuzzy greets me with a bear hug, and an even more enveloping smile, and if the weather is decent, he may suggest a golf game. He demands "three strokes a side" for the cancer that several years ago stripped him of his larynx. His makeshift "voice box" makes him sound as raspy artificially as I sound naturally.

Marv Fleming, the tight end, the first man to play in five Super Bowls, two with the Packers and three with Miami, is, unofficially, my adopted seventh child. Marv is in his fifties, only seven or eight years younger than me, but he seems to believe he is still an adolescent, and often acts the part, convincingly. A lifelong bachelor who has a high, squeaky voice and claims to be the first NFL player to wear an earring, Marvin has been labeled, in print, a "gay" athlete, which amuses him and confounds the women he has always dated. Marv is a part-time spokesman for the ski slopes of Park City, Utah, and each year, when my family enjoys a skiing trip at the end of winter, he serves as our volunteer instructor and companion, especially at dinnertime. Marvin loves free meals; he is monumentally frugal, and proud of it.

Max McGee, the wide receiver, is monumentally generous when he and his wife Denise come to New York and entertain my wife and me. Denise loves the theater, and Max good food and vintage wines. We have dined on classic French food at Lutèce, and we have toasted Bobby Short, the piano player who lights up the Cafe Carlyle. Once, when the McGees and the Schaaps were standing at a bar, my wife, suffering from hypoglycemia at the time, grew dizzy and fainted. As she slid toward the floor, McGee, who reached back to make a spectacular one-handed catch on his way to the first touchdown in Super Bowl history, reached out to catch her—and missed. My wife slipped through McGee's sure hands.

I was privileged to deliver one of the eulogies at the funeral in Appleton, Wisconsin, of Ron Kostelnik, the defensive tackle, one of the three Super Bowl I Packers who died before Super Bowl XXXI. On happier occasions, I attended the wedding in Madison of Ron's son, Mike, and Ron's widow Peggy helped us observe my daughter Kari's bat mitzvah in New York.

I have traveled to Louisville to appear on a TV show that is hosted by Paul Hornung, the halfback, and I have invaded Montana to risk whitewater rafting on the Yellowstone River with Jimmy Taylor, the fullback. I have conducted interviews in the New Jersey condo of Herb Adderley, the cornerback, and the Alabama office of Bart Starr, the quarterback.

I love to listen to Dave Robinson, the linebacker, when he laughs and pokes fun at his own considerable girth—"When I told my wife I lost ten pounds, she said, 'That's like throwing a deck chair off the *Titanic*' "—and I love to listen to Willie Davis, the defensive end, when he reasons and reflects and then speaks, as thoughtful an athlete as I've known, next to Arthur Ashe.

I've been to the homes of Red Mack, a scrappy journeyman who played his final NFL game in Super Bowl I, and Bob Skoronski, the tackle who captained the Packer offense with little fanfare and less error. I've roamed the sprawling 26,000-acre Texas ranch run by Tommy Joe Crutcher, the linebacker; I joined Kramer and Kostelnik and Doug Hart, the cornerback, and Lee Roy Caffey, the linebacker, and Donny Anderson, the halfback, as they hunted birds and played poker only a few miles from the Mexican border. I've played golf with Willie Wood, the safety, and attended speeches by Lionel Aldridge, the defensive end and paranoid schizophrenic who is candid about his continuing struggle for mental health. I visited Bill Curry, the center, in Tuscaloosa when he coached the University of Alabama, and I participate each year in a Memphis golf tournament dedicated to the memory of Steve Bratkowski, the son of Zeke Bratkowski, the backup quarterback.

The walls of my office at ABC News are hung with

photos of Lombardi's Packers in action—Hornung diving across a goal line, Kostelnik menacing a quarterback, McGee taunting a defender—and in repose. Ray Nitschke's face, fierce even in his fifties, stares down and still intimidates me. Only Muhammad Ali, whom I have known even longer than I have known Paul Hornung, his fellow Louisvillian, commands as much space as the Packers on my wall. Lombardi's people are my friends and my contemporaries; Starr and Davis and I were born the same year, Thurston the previous year, Hornung the next.

Once, in 1989, when the NCAA's Final Four converged in Seattle, I invited Vince Lombardi, the son, who was practicing law in the city, to join me for dinner with the Indiana basketball coach, Bob Knight. The two men had never met, and when I introduced them to each other, I said, "Vince Lombardi Junior, this is Vince Lombardi Junior." I thought it was a pretty clever remark. Neither of them laughed.

I do not pretend to know the Packers of the 1990s so well as I know their ancestors, but early in their super season of 1996, I was struck by the growing bond between them and their predecessors, the mutual respect of two generations of football players. I decided then that I wanted to write a book about the new Packers, and the old, and the connections, large and small, direct and coincidental, that drew them together. I was willing to gamble that the season would turn out well, and Avon Books, the publisher, agreed to bankroll my gamble.

I made half a dozen pilgrimages to Green Bay in the

fall and winter of 1996–1997 and got to know many of the current players at least casually. I'd known Jim McMahon, the backup quarterback, for more than a decade and long suspected, from his rudeness and arrogance, that he might be the biggest asshole in the NFL. Imagine my surprise when, suddenly, in the fall of 1996, at the start of his first full season as a Packer, McMahon turned amiable, even charming. Green Bay must have rubbed off on him.

My secretary, Jeanne Collins, grew up in New Jersey with George Winters, the father of Frank Winters, the Packers' center, and through Jeanne, I met George before I met his son. George is even larger than Frank, a booming, gregarious man whom I liked immediately. In New Orleans, at the annual Super Bowl Eve party that my wife and I host, George Winters and his wife represented the new Packers. Kramer, Hornung, McGee, Thurston, Boyd Dowler, and Peggy Kostelnik Spaulding represented the old.

Through Frank, I got to know his two best friends in Green Bay, his teammates Mark Chmura, the tight end, and Brett Favre, the quarterback, and one afternoon in New Orleans, the four of us started out to drive to nearby Kiln, Mississippi, Favre's hometown. Strangely enough, we got only as far as a local branch of Hooters, an outpost on the perimeter of the French Quarter. We spent close to four hours in Hooters, thinking football, I'm sure, and exceeding my drinking limit, which is approximately two beers. Favre started with Diet Pepsi, then switched to ice water. Chmura and Winters and I opted for more conventional fare.

In small ways, I tried to bridge the generation gap with a handful of the current Packers, to relax them, to encourage them to share thoughts and memories. Eugene Robinson, the free safety, and I talked over lunch about going to college in upstate New York; we discussed Adonal Foyle, the young basketball star at Colgate, Eugene's alma mater. Derrick Mayes, the rookie receiver, and I talked about Crispus Attucks High School in Indianapolis; his mother was now the principal, and I could recall when the star of the Attucks basketball team was Oscar Robertson, and the coach was Ray Crowe. Marco Rivera, a rookie guard, and I talked of our roots in Brooklyn and our backgrounds in lacrosse. Sean Jones, the defensive end, and I talked of mutual friends at the Center for the Study of Sport in Society at Northeastern University, his alma mater—he got a real degree; I'm delighted to be getting an honorary one—and Sean offered the thoughtful suggestion that my son, a correspondent for ESPN, ought to wear more tasteful ties.

I looked upon Reggie White with special affection. Early in 1996, when the Packers were only a victory over Dallas away from going to the Super Bowl, I was in Green Bay, working on a story, interviewing Reggie, and when I mentioned that I was experiencing nagging pain in my right knee, he said that he would pray for me. I thanked White, who is an ordained minister, and assumed that he meant that on Sunday he would pray for me in church.

But Reggie had more immediate plans. He went to the Packer locker room and soon returned with Keith

Jackson, the tight end, and a small jar of ointment. Reggie rubbed a bit of the ointment onto my forehead, and then he and Keith kneeled in front of me, bowed their heads, and began praying aloud for my knee. Their sincerity was obvious, and I was so moved, so touched that, perhaps in a rush of adrenaline, the pain in my knee subsided.

I thanked Reggie and Keith for their kindness. They went off to practice.

Fifteen minutes later, my knee remembered it was Jewish, and began to throb again.

Still, I was grateful for even the brief respite.

And as the 1996 Green Bay Packers flourished, faltered in midseason, and revived, I openly rooted for them to go to New Orleans, to play in Super Bowl XXXI, and to win it. I had a vested interest, financially and emotionally, and I confess I cheered for the young Packers to become world champions almost as enthusiastically as their most ardent fans, their most knowledgeable supporters, the old world champions, the Green Bay Packers who played for Vince Lombardi.

BOOK ONE

THE GHOSTS OF THE TUNDRA

Green Bay vs. Carolina

January 12, 1997

Ghosts walk the state of Wisconsin. The Ridgeway Phantom prowls the woods of Iowa County in the southwest corner of the state, sometimes assuming human form, sometimes animal. Not far away, in Mineral Point, the murderer William Caffey headlessly haunts the aging inn where he was hanged a century and a half ago. Across the state, the spectral explorer ship *Griffin*, which vanished three hundred years ago after being cursed by an Iroquois prophet, occasionally flickers in the fog in Green Bay Harbor.

Wisconsin is home to "more ghosts per square mile than any state in the union," a University of Wisconsin professor named Robert Gard once wrote, and nowhere are those ghosts more concentrated, or more consecrated, than in a mid–twentieth century structure called Lambeau Field, a monument perched on Lombardi Avenue, precisely where Green Bay, Wisconsin, goes bump against neighboring Ashwaubenon.

Curly Lambeau and Vince Lombardi, football coaches by profession, are only two of the apparitions who haunt the stadium and street that bear their names. They are conventional ghosts, in the sense that both are officially dead. Lambeau died in 1965, and Lombardi, who was only fifty-seven, five years later. Most of the other specters of Green Bay are, oxymoronically, living ghosts. Bart Starr, for instance, is very much alive, and so are Paul Hornung and Willie Davis and Willie Wood, all of whom happened to materialize at Lambeau Field on Lombardi Avenue on January 12, 1997.

They appeared, along with several of their fellow football shades from the sixties, to attend the annual National Football Conference championship game and celebrate slightly tardily the twenty-ninth anniversary of the Wisconsin version of the Battle of Hastings, the aptly named Ice Bowl. Schoolchildren in Green Bay and Ashwaubenon learn December 31, 1967, long before they learn 1066.

On that historic year-ending date, the Green Bay Packers, a football team owned and worshipped by the local community, played the Dallas Cowboys for the championship of the National Football League, the winner to meet the champions of the American Football League in Super Bowl II two weeks later in Miami. (The following year, incidentally, the members of the National Football League changed the name of their gaggle to the National Football *Conference*, the members of the American Football League switched theirs to the American Football *Conference*, and those designations, despite a little juggling, a few teams added and a few relocated, have persisted.)

On January 12, 1997, the Green Bay Packers were meeting the Carolina Panthers for the NFC championship and the right to represent the conference in Super Bowl XXXI two weeks later in New Orleans. Only two of the Packers, the veterans Jim McMahon and Don Beebe, passer and receiver, had ever played in a Super Bowl. Only McMahon, playing for the Chicago Bears eleven years earlier, had ever won one. Beebe had played for the Buffalo Bills, who went to four straight Super Bowls in the early 1990s and lost four straight Super Bowls. Outside of the Super Bowl, and an affection for backgammon and golf, McMahon, a brash hell-raiser, and Beebe, a born-again Christian, had very few experiences in common.

Reggie White, thirty-five years old, in his twelfth NFL season, had never played in a Super Bowl. He is a gentle giant of a defensive end, a contradiction in many ways, a minister off the field, a marauder on the field, striving simultaneously to sack quarterbacks and to save them. "I see his eyes on game day," says Max McGee, the Super Bowl I hero who now broadcasts Packer games. "He's ready to play. He doesn't look like a minister then."

A man-child, naïve yet sincere, White is not phony, not a hypocrite. He does not pretend to be holier than thou or me or anyone else. Reggie walks the walk. He is also one of the great defensive players in the history of the NFL. "Reggie's a throwback," Ray Nitschke, the old linebacker, says. "He could play in any era."

Brett Favre, twenty-seven years old, in his sixth NFL season, had never played in a Super Bowl. Favre is a Mississippian, a good old boy, given to country sayings and country ways. "Shit be bringin' it, hoss," was his mantra during the 1996 season, his response to almost every situation. Who knows exactly what it meant. But don't think Favre is dumb, not for a moment. He is quick and clever, on the field and off. He is also the best quarterback in football, the Most Valuable Player in the NFL two years in a row. "I've never seen a quarterback who possessed so much talent at this stage of his career," Bart Starr insists. Only one man before Favre had repeated as MVP, Joe Montana of the San Francisco 49ers, and that was after Montana had served in the NFL for ten seasons. Still, Favre shies away from comparisons with Montana. "No way I'm even close to him," Favre says.

White, anchoring the defense, and Favre, igniting the offense, are clearly the leaders of the Packers. Ask each member of the team the key to its success, and half would say Reggie and half would say Brett, and Reggie would say Brett and Brett would say Reggie, and if that mutual admiration, that suppressing of ego, doesn't go a long way toward explaining the Packers' success, nothing does. Personally, Reggie and Brett are about as far apart as Beebe and McMahon; professionally, they share a devotion to winning.

Reggie and Brett and their fifty-one Packer teammates spent the night before the NFC championship game in Green Bay's Radisson Hotel, across the road from the airport and adjacent to the thriving Oneida Casino. In the morning, after breakfast, the players split into two groups for chapel services, the Protestants led by the regional director of Athletes in Action, the self-annointed team chaplain, Steve Newman, and the Catholics by Father John Blaha, known as "The Packer Priest," who also helped out in the equipment room and ran on the field to retrieve the kicking tee during games.

"There is nothing about the Packers that is going to give you eternal life," Father Blaha once confessed. "There is nothing about the Packers that will grant you forgiveness of sin." Still, Father Blaha has left instructions that someday, "I am to be buried in a standard casket wearing my priestly vestments. And underneath that I am to be wearing a Packers T-shirt. . . ."

Most of the black Packers, including Reggie, attended the Protestant services. Most of the white Packers, including Brett, attended the Catholic services. Protestants, and blacks, outnumbered Catholics, and whites, almost precisely two to one. There were crossovers: Santana Dotson, a black defensive tackle, lined up with the Catholics; Adam Timmerman, a white offensive guard, beefed up the Protestants.

Interestingly, only two of the white Packers, Mike Prior and Bob Kuberski, played defense. The rest were kickers and quarterbacks, runners, receivers, and offensive linemen.

*   *   *

The first black Packer was Nate Borden, who arrived in Green Bay in 1955 and once borrowed Max McGee's car and drove it, not deliberately, through the window of a furniture store. "Well, Nate," said McGee, when he learned of the mishap, "how much furniture did we buy?"

Borden was joined, in his final Green Bay season, which was Vince Lombardi's first, by Emlen Tunnell, a veteran safety whose career as a New York Giant earned him a place in the Pro Football Hall of Fame. Tunnell came to Green Bay with Lombardi. At the time, Tunnell used to say, the only black people in Green Bay were he and Borden and the porter in the old Northland Hotel. Tunnell lived in the hotel; Borden lived in a hovel. Lombardi pilloried his landlord and found Borden a decent place to live.

Green Bay's minuscule black population multiplied as fast as Lombardi was able to acquire such players as Willie Davis, Willie Wood, Herb Adderley, Lionel Aldridge, Marv Fleming, Dave Robinson, Elijah Pitts, Travis Williams, Bob Jeter, Bob Brown, and more. Lombardi did not tolerate intolerance. "If I ever hear anyone using any racial epithets around here like nigger or dago or kike," he told his players, "you're gone, I don't care who you are."

Once, when a talented white player, angry because a black teammate had beaten him out for the All-Pro team, fortified himself with a few drinks, then called Lombardi and demanded to know, "How come that nigger made the team and I didn't?" Lombardi cut him from the squad.

"When I got to the Packers," Dave Robinson remembers, "there were only nine black players on the team, and two of them were named Willie. So, if a guy saw you downtown and yelled, 'Hey, Willie,' more than twenty percent of the time he'd be right. We laughed about it. We knew the people in Green Bay knew we were football players and wanted to say 'Hello' to us, wanted to say *something*. So they said, 'Willie.' They didn't mean anything derogatory by it."

In the twenty-nine years and twelve days—but who's counting?—between surviving the Ice Bowl and confronting Carolina, the Green Bay Packers had never won an NFC championship game, had never even played one in Green Bay. The team and its fans had experienced an agonizingly lengthy drought.

In the first quarter of a century after the Ice Bowl, in twenty-five years of football, the Packers had managed only five winning seasons, qualified for the playoffs only twice, and won only a single postseason game. It was a cruel awakening for a team and town that had been spoiled by five NFL championships in the previous seven seasons, an unprecedented and unmatched splurge.

In November 1996, when Bill Clinton outpolled Bob Dole in Brown County—Green Bay is the county seat—the Green Bay *Press-Gazette* noted that it was the first time since Lyndon Johnson in 1964 that a Democratic Presidential candidate had carried the county. "The Democrats' dry spell," the *Press-Gazette* reported, putting things in perspective, "surpassed even the Packers' lengthy absence from the Super Bowl."

The *Press-Gazette* did not see fit to print another significant tie between the Packers and Presidential politics. In their mostly glorious history, the Packers had won the NFL championship game eight times: three victories with Franklin Roosevelt in the White House, two with John F. Kennedy, and three with Lyndon Johnson. The Packers had never won an NFL championship game with a Republican in the White House (although they had won three NFL titles, before the introduction of championship games, when Herbert Hoover held the national reins). Had the *Press-Gazette* even hinted at this tidbit of trivia before Election Day 1996, Dole probably would have lost Brown County by a considerably more decisive margin.

Bill Clinton brought his reelection campaign to Green Bay during the first week of the 1996 NFL season. He delivered a Labor Day speech in nearby De Pere, then informed his staff, "I want to see Lambeau Field." The President was escorted to the stadium, shook hands with Bob Harlan, Ron Wolf, and Mike Holmgren, the president, general manager, and head coach of the Packers, talked to the players, posed for photographs, looked up at the empty stands, and said, on behalf of the sports fans of the United States, "Boy, I never thought I'd get a chance to see this place!"

Clinton was only the third American President to set eyes on Lambeau Field while he was in office. A pair of Republicans, Presidents Ford and Nixon, preceded him, Ford to dedicate the Green Bay Packers Hall of Fame in 1976, Nixon to celebrate Bart Starr Day six years earlier. Both were former football players. Ford played center at Michigan; Nixon played end at Whittier and quarterback at Watergate.

Two previous Presidential visits had nothing to do with football. Franklin D. Roosevelt showed up in 1934 to observe the tercentennial of Jean Nicolet's landing on the shores of Green Bay (known for a time as "La Baie des Puants," the Bay of the Stinking Water), the first white man to set foot in the territory that eventually became Wisconsin. Nicolet, who had sailed through the Great Lakes from Canada, was not exactly delighted to find land. He had been hoping to find a waterway to China. William Howard Taft, the Gilbert Brown of Presidents, gave a speech on the steps of the Brown County Courthouse in 1911, long before the Packers (or, for that matter, Gilbert Brown, their 350-pound defensive lineman) were conceived.

Candidates Eisenhower, Kennedy, Carter, Reagan, and Bush all campaigned in Green Bay before they won the Presidency. When President-to-be Zachary Taylor was a young army officer, he commanded Fort Howard, the military post, built early in the nineteenth century, that overlooked the Fox River and guarded northeastern Wisconsin. After he was transferred to a western Wisconsin post in Prairie du Chien, Taylor's daughter ran off with a young lieutenant in his command. The young lieutenant also became President, the only President of the Confederacy, Jefferson Davis.

On December 31, 1967, on the brink of a New Year and Lyndon B. Johnson's last full year in the White House, the temperature in Lambeau Field at game time, 1:11 P.M. Central Standard Time, was 13 degrees below zero, and the wind-chill factor—a northwest wind scudded through the stands at 15 miles an hour—drove the temperature down to 45 below. Ideal weather, for an Ice Bowl.

I remember driving from my motel to downtown Green Bay that morning and passing a sign outside a bank that blinked the time and the temperature. It was shortly before ten, and the temperature was twelve below. I had never heard of twelve below. I assumed the thermometer was broken.

Twenty-nine years later, the preferences of network television determined that nothing would be finer than for the Packers to meet Carolina in the morning, at 11:35 A.M. Green Bay time, 12:35 P.M. Madison Avenue time. The AFC championship game, matching New England and Jacksonville, could then be safely scheduled for a few minutes after 4:00 P.M. Eastern Standard Time, leaving time for postgame ceremonies and postmortems, perhaps even an overtime session if sudden-death were required.

Green Bay fans, and a heavily outnumbered force of Panther partisans, began streaming toward the stadium at dawn, and by breakfast time for saner folk, the parking lots surrounding Lambeau Field were filled with cars and fans ablaze in green and gold and the sweet-and-sour smells of bratwurst and beer. Packer fans do not *always* drink before noon, but Sunday rituals must be observed, and tailgating is among the more compelling, even when the Packers play a morning game. After all, no one under thirty had ever previously tailgated before a championship game at Lambeau.

Green Bay is an industrial town of barely 100,000 people, predominantly white-skinned and blue-collared, a town of smoke stacks and steeples and saloons. The people embrace old-fashioned values; most of them believe in a day's work for a day's pay, and even the ones who don't seem to admire the ones who do. They tend to be friendly, honest, straightforward people who don't put much stock in frills and fanciness. They are fiercely proud of their Packers.

And they are *their* Packers. The people tailgating in the parking lot not only cheer for the team; they *own* the team. Farmers own the team, and factory workers, lawyers and shopkeepers, housewives and nurses, 1,915 of them. Among them, they own 4,634 shares of stocks. Each share once cost twenty-five dollars and is now worth nothing, or everything. The stock can't be traded. There are no dividends. Not even any perks; some of the owners can't buy tickets to the Packers' games. This is the only publicly owned nonprofit big-league sports franchise in the United States, and maybe in the world, which is why the worthless stock is so valuable. Millionaires dream of owning one share. "Next to my wife and kids," says a stockholder named Jim Queoff, "it's my most valued possession."

*   *   *

By 9:00 A.M., the Packers began trickling into their locker room. They cut from their special parking lot through the gymnasium and the weight room, then crossed a hallway lined with eleven banners, green with gold lettering, each commemorating one of the Packers' NFL championships. Inside the locker room, players sat in various states of undress, staring, thinking, putting on their game faces. Normally mild men—William Henderson, the fullback, and Craig Newsome, the cornerback, for instance—metamorphosed into warriors. Several players clustered around two long tables. One table was for backgammon games, the other for dominos. Most of the backgammon players were Catholics who played offense. Most of the domino players were Protestants who played defense. Eugene Robinson, the free safety, older and more thoughtful than most of his teammates, preferred the challenge of crossword puzzles.

Many of the Packers sat with headsets plugged into their skulls, absorbing their favorite music. Once there had almost been a war over locker-room music among the Protestants who played defense. Reggie White championed gospel music; Wayne Simmons, a linebacker and provocateur, favored gangsta sounds. When White demanded that Simmons tune out the rap, and Simmons responded with a burst of profanity, Reggie objected to both the words and the music. The two men almost came to blows. During the final two months of the 1996 season, just about the only music that could be safely played on a boom box in the locker room was a Bob Marley CD. Even the Catholics who played offense liked that one.

In the last official census in 1990, there were 453 black Americans in Green Bay, less than one-half of 1 percent of the population. Not only whites outnumbered blacks; so did Native Americans, Hispanics, and Asians. There were more blacks, however, than Tongans, Eskimos, Cambodians, Malayans, and Bangladeshi, of which there was one apiece.

Understandably, a young black man in Green Bay is presumed to be a Packer, especially if he has a large and muscular frame or an exotic car, unless he proves otherwise. And, just as understandably, many of those young men do not enjoy being asked, repeatedly, "Which one are you?"

"You can see them whispering, 'Which one is he?' " Antonio Freeman, the wide receiver, says. "But you can't look at it in a negative way. We're celebrities. We're superstars to the people in this area."

In some cities, a young black man driving an expensive car is presumed too often to be a drug dealer, which is harsh and flagrant racism. Being called a Packer is a lot better.

Paul Hornung and Willie Wood were among the early arrivals at Lambeau, and not just to check out their names among the nineteen that are emblazoned on the green walls between the two floors of private stadium boxes leased (at about $20,000 a box annually) by the warm and the wealthy. The names—ten on the west wall, nine on the east—are of the nineteen Packer players and coaches who have been inducted into the Pro Football Hall of Fame. In Green Bay, ghosts get billing.

Lombardi is one of the nineteen; ten of the others are men who played for him. Seven of them—Starr, Nitschke, Adderley, Davis, Wood, Forrest Gregg, and Henry Jordan—played in the Ice Bowl; Hornung, who had retired from football that season, sat on the Packers' bench during the Ice Bowl, usurping a perch near the heater. The popular Hornung's presence, which required the permission of Commissioner Pete Rozelle, warmed his teammates' hearts, if not their bodies.

Hornung and Wood had returned to Green Bay for the NFC title game at the request of Ron Wolf, the general manager, who had asked them to serve as honorary co-captains. Wolf and the head coach, Mike Holmgren, both students of football history and tradition, both fascinated and thrilled and haunted by the Packer past, had instituted the practice of honorary captains to link the past and the present, to forge a bond between Lombardi's people and theirs.

Ron Kostelnik had served as the first honorary captain, in the opening game of 1992, two-and-a-half years before he died of a heart attack. Since then, every living Hall of Famer except one, and several lesser players, had served as an honorary captain. The one exception was Forrest Gregg, the offensive tackle Lombardi once called "the finest player I've ever coached."

Gregg, who lasted sixteen seasons in the NFL and once played in 188 consecutive games, coached the Packers for four seasons in the 1980s, an unsuccessful tour that ended so acrimoniously Wolf feared that a decade later Gregg might still be booed.

Wood and Hornung walked the playing field before the game, so buoyed by the occasion that Hornung, who never lacked self-confidence, threatened to attempt a Lambeau Leap. The maneuever was invented in 1993 by LeRoy Butler, the strong safety who, after returning a fumble for his first NFL touchdown, decided to jump into the stands, into the cushioning arms of grateful Packer fans. Butler didn't quite get high enough to make it all the way into the seats, but two years later Robert Brooks, the wide receiver, emulated and improved Butler's move. Since then, a dozen different Packers, primarily receivers and running backs, including, once, a tandem of ball carriers, had attempted the leap; none, however, of Hornung's age or girth (except, of course, the tandem).

"Willie," Hornung called, "I'm gonna jump in."

"If you do," Wood responded, "it's gonna be in slow motion."

Hornung sprinted toward the wall. Would you believe *jogged? Ambled?* Then he *soared* perhaps half an inch off the ground. "I'm not crazy," Hornung said. "You have to turn around and jump backward. I could've ruined my golf game." He could've crushed a fan.

(The Packers, logically, discourage their players from

performing the Leap during road games. Landing in hostile laps is just too risky.)

Wood and Hornung were only two of the ghosts patrolling Lambeau. It was logical that Willie Davis, owner of four radio stations in Milwaukee and California, a member of the board of directors of MGM/United Artists and K-Mart and half a dozen other major corporations, a millionaire businessman and civic leader, was also present. Davis is one of three former Packers who sits on the team's unpaid forty-five man Board of Directors.

And it was inevitable that Bart Starr, who runs a flourishing business developing and operating medical office buildings, showed up. Even though Starr had not succeeded when he came back to coach in Green Bay, even though his teams had never won more than eight games in any of his nine seasons, even though he was fired six days before Christmas 1983, Starr still feels tremendous loyalty to the team, to the city, and, perhaps most of all, to the coach who had nurtured his career.

Of all the connections between Lombardi's Packers and Holmgren's, none seem so striking as the parallels between quarterbacks Bart Starr and Brett Favre, and between defensive ends Willie Davis and Reggie White. The kinship goes far beyond their positions and the ring of their names.

They come from similar backgrounds: Bart and Brett were born in the neighboring Southern states of Alabama and Mississippi ("Just a couple of Bubbas," Starr says); Willie and Reggie grew up in the neighboring Southern states of Arkansas and Tennessee. Neither Bart nor Brett was a blue-chip prospect coming out of college. The Packers picked Starr in the seventeenth round of the draft in 1956. The Atlanta Falcons picked Favre in the second round of the draft in 1991 (quarterbacks Dan McGwire and Todd Marinovich were drafted ahead of him). In his rookie season, Brett did not complete a single pass; he threw only five. In Starr's rookie season, he threw only forty-four passes, completed twenty-four. They both took control of Green Bay teams that were losers and helped transform them into winners.

Davis and White, like Starr and Favre, are linked by their football skills and by leadership qualities that transcend the game. When Davis earned his M.B.A. from the University of Chicago, the dean of the business school, George Schultz, who later served as President Reagan's secretary of state, said, "In whatever setting you place Willie Davis, he will be a leader. People pay attention to him." The Reverend White commands attention, too.

Reggie regrets that he never encountered Davis's mentor, Vince Lombardi. "I would have loved to have sat down and talked to him," White told me one day. "His sayings were some of the greatest sayings I've ever heard from a coach. He didn't sound like a coach. He sounded like a preacher." From Reggie, that is the ultimate compliment.

Davis is impressed, in turn, by the way Reggie White

raised the level of racial consciousness among Packer fans, partly just by his presence and partly by the attention drawn to the burning early in 1996 of the Inner City Community Church, the Tennessee church White served as assistant minister. "He made the people of Green Bay aware of the aspirations and the frustrations of African-Americans," Davis says.

(Coincidentally, Reggie White was born twelve days before the Packers won the first of their five NFL titles in seven years. In the first twenty-five months of Reggie's life, the Packers won twenty-seven games and lost only three. His contributions to those victories were minimal.)

"Reggie is one of the greatest players ever," Willie Davis says. "I don't know why they had to bring in a guy that good to play the same position I played."

Starr and Favre met the first year the younger quarterback came to Green Bay and immediately took to each other. 'When I met Bart," Favre says, "I had no clue what Green Bay football was all about. He kind of filled me in."

"I correspond with Brett," Starr says. "I like him. I like his courage, his toughness, his ability. This young man is a complete quarterback."

Starr was not a bad quarterback himself, the Most Valuable Player in two Super Bowls, the Packers' starter for thirteen of his sixteen seasons. "Truthfully," he says, "I was an overachiever. Brett's not. He's a talent."

"I haven't done close to what Bart Starr has done,"

Favre counters. "If I'd done what Bart has done, I'd be bigger than Elvis."

Of all Favre's strengths, the one Starr admires most is his toughness. "You can have all of the other assets going for you," Bart says, "but when you're facing a great defense in a crucial game, toughness becomes paramount. The champion quarterbacks all possess it. Those that don't win somehow can't muster it."

"You pride yourself on being tough?" I once asked him.

"Yes," Bart Starr said, quietly. "I know you can't win without it."

Bart Starr is a proven winner, a consistent winner who, in his life, suffered perhaps only one great loss. In 1988, Bart found his twenty-four-year-old son dead, killed by cocaine abuse. The boy's name was Bret. Bret Starr.

Brett Favre knows the taste of tragedy, too. During training camp in 1996, his best friend from Mississippi, Mark Haverty, died in a car crash; Brett's brother, Scott, who was driving, was charged with being under the influence. A month later, Brett's sister Brandi, a former Miss Teen Mississippi, was a passenger in a car involved in a drive-by shooting. Favre had to cope with his friend's death, and his siblings' crises, while he confronted his own problem, an addiction he had developed to Vicodin, a painkiller of choice for many football players.

Football players need painkillers the way performers

need makeup, to camouflage the wounds or flaws that might force them to move or think or react less swiftly, less productively. If they are wise, they use the pain-killers sensibly and sparingly. If they are quarterbacks, their need often escalates into demand. There are so many hits, so many bruises, so many decisions to make and actions to take. In 1995, no quarterback in the NFL made so many good moves, mentally and physically, as Brett Favre. Few took a greater pounding; his ankles, knees, shoulders, ribs, and back all ached almost constantly. And, quite possibly, no quarterback devoured more painkillers. Teammates knew, and so did coaches, and they worried about him. But Brett Favre was the MVP. Obviously, he knew what he was doing.

He didn't. He was out of control. He took thirteen Vicodin pills one night, and that was *after* the season was over. His live-in girlfriend, his friend since high school, Deanna Tynnes, sometimes flushed his pills down the toilet. She was terrified. "I worried he was going to die," she said.

On February 27, 1996, Favre almost did. He was in Green Bay's Bellin Hospital, recuperating from ankle surgery, talking to Deanna and their seven-year-old daughter, Brittany, when, suddenly, he suffered a sei-zure, which may have been induced by Vicodin. Favre says it wasn't; he also says that he wasn't frightened. But everyone around him was, and Brett may have be-gun to understand that, despite the Superman tattoo high on his left arm, he was mortal.

Still, Favre hesitated, rationalized, delayed until May announcing that he was entering the Menninger

Clinic, the famous rehabilitation center in Topeka, Kansas. He was going to battle his addiction to painkillers, his affinity for alcohol. Favre had spent many nights scrambling from bar to bar in Green Bay, a world-class drinker in a world-class drinking town. He was not an alcoholic, but he was far more than a social drinker.

The night he announced he was going to Menninger, Favre called Reggie White, who told him that his decision took more courage than anything he had ever done on the football field.

Favre is honest about his rehabilitation. "First of all, I didn't want to do it," he admits. "Second, I didn't want to have it go public. It's a personal problem, and people don't want personal problems to be out in the open. But I knew I had to do it, and I knew I had to go public. Otherwise, the rumors would've been much worse than the truth. And I knew that once I went public, I had to make a strong commitment to beat this and be a better person off the field, a better player on the field.

"People were going to be eyeing every little thing I did. There's no way of being perfect, but I had to try to be perfect."

Favre spent forty-six days at the Menninger Clinic. His friends, his family, and his team were all supportive. Frank Winters, who lives in Overland Park, Kansas, during the off-season, visited him often enough to get to know several of Brett's fellow patients. Mike Holmgren visited him, and so did Deanna. Soon after Brett came out, he married Deanna.

During the 1996 football season, Favre was sacked forty times and hit perhaps four hundred. Once, against Denver, he was hit so hard he played a full quarter in a trance. He went all season without a single Vicodin or a single drink. He took nothing stronger than Tylenol and Motrin. "The bottom line," he said, "is that sometimes you've got to play in pain. This isn't badminton. It's football. Guys try to kill each other."

To almost everyone's surprise, except his own, he played even better in 1996 than he had played in 1995. He wasn't perfect, but he was close.

"I am pretty proud of myself," Brett told me.

Jerry Kramer came from Idaho to see the Carolina game. Several months earlier, Kramer had been nominated for the Pro Football Hall of Fame. He had been proposed by the Seniors Committee, a subcommittee of five of the Hall's thirty-six member Board of Selectors. The recommendation of the Seniors Committee usually led to election by the full board. Kramer would find out on January 25, 1997, the day before Super Bowl XXXI, if he would join his Ice Bowl teammates on the Lambeau Wall of Fame. "I think he deserves it," said Bob Harlan, the Packers' president. "Jerry should've been in before me," Paul Hornung said. "He defined his position."

Max McGee came from Minneapolis to broadcast the game on WTMJ in Milwaukee, the flagship of the fifty-eight stations on the Packer radio network. McGee had been offering colorful commentary to Packer fans for seventeen years, broadcasting for the fun of it, not the money. In the 1970s, McGee started ChiChi's, the Tex-Mex restaurant chain, then sold his share for more than $10 million. He next invested in casinos on Indian reservations, and his earnings as an investor outnumbered his losses at the craps table by several more millions. "If the Packers win the Super Bowl this year, I'll retire," McGee threatened. "If they don't, I'll be back."

Fuzzy Thurston came from his Green Bay saloon to cheer for the Packers, and Ray Nitschke from his nearby home to prod them. Thurston had become the team's ultimate cheerleader, Nitschke the ultimate surrogate coach, a stand-in Lombardi.

The week leading up to the Carolina game, Thurston was so pumped up, he said he felt like a fifteen-year-old. A few nights before the NFC title match, he crouched down in a three-point stance in the icy parking lot of a local restaurant and offered to block my rented car. "I'll be on top of the world," Fuzzy said, "when the Packers win the Super Bowl."

"Ray's really intense," Reggie White said. "He'll come over and smack you in the face and say, 'You can't lose this game.' He's like a coach, but after a while you say, 'Ray, you got to stop smacking me.' "

Nitschke, Thurston, McGee, Kramer, Starr, Davis, Hornung, Wood. That made eight men on hand from the Lombardi era, from the so-called "Glory Years," eight-and-a-half counting Gary Knafelc, a wide receiver who put in five years in Green Bay before Lombardi, then four years under Lombardi. Knafelc, now the public-address announcer at Lambeau, scored the winning touchdown in the first game played in the stadium, in 1957.

*   *   *

Green Bay experienced a championship drought before Lombardi as well as after Lombardi. After beating the New York Giants for the NFL title in 1944, the Packers turned in three marginally successful seasons under Curly Lambeau, then slid into eleven straight years without a winning record. After the first two of those unhappy years, 3–9 and 2–10 disasters, Lambeau stepped down as head coach. Curly had coached the Packers for the first thirty-one years of their existence, and until his final years of 1948 and 1949, he had endured only one losing season, in 1933. The Packers emerged from that momentary depression faster than the country did.

But the depression that preceded Lombardi was a major one—fourteen years without a title when he showed up, the last eleven seasons in a row at .500 or lower. The team bottomed out in 1958. The Pulitzer Prize–winning columnist, Red Smith of the New York *Herald Tribune*, perhaps the most gifted of all American sportswriters, reported that the 1958 Packers "overwhelmed one opponent, underwhelmed ten and whelmed one." Those clever words were not pleasant for Smith to pen. After all, like Lambeau, Smith was born in Green Bay, and, like Lambeau, Smith went from East High School to college at Notre Dame. Red, who was seven years younger, saw Lambeau play at East High and in the NFL.

Smith also had ties to Vince Lombardi, who, before he took over the Packers, was an assistant coach at West Point and with the New York Giants. Smith frequently covered both Army and the Giants for the *Herald Tribune*. Lombardi, his friend once wrote, "was inwardly as violent as a crime of passion."

On the final day of 1961, in his hometown, Smith watched Lombardi's revitalized Packers destroy the New York Giants, 37–0, for the first of their five championships in the sixties. Drawing upon his considerable local knowledge, Smith wrote, "Back around 1634 when the big outdoor game in these parts was lacrosse, a victory for the Menominees over the Sacs was celebrated by tribal dancing, drinking and yelling all night like one in despair. After three centuries and more, things haven't changed a lick, except that pro football has moved in as the most popular spectator sport . . .

". . . the mighty Packers," Smith continued, "simply slathered New York's hapless Giants yesterday to give their untamed electorate its first National League championship in seventeen years, and the best excuse for the New Year's Day wobblies since squaws learned to squeeze the juice from corn."

It is, of course, enormously fitting that the two most famous people ever born in Green Bay were Walter "Red" Smith and Earl "Curly" Lambeau, a sportswriter and a football coach. A longtime Congressman named John W. Byrnes and a *Wall Street Journal* journalist named Paul Gigot duel for a distant third place.

Gary Knafelc remembers that in 1958, Dad Braisher, the Packers' equipment manager, used to clean up the locker room after games so that the players and their families would have a place to go Sunday nights, a place where they could unwind, enjoy a beer and a brat, listen to a juke box, and lick their wounds. It was no fun, in 1958, being seen in public after playing a game in a Packer uniform. There were unsold seats at Packer games in 1958 and in 1959, and never since.

The roller-coaster history of the Packers can be summed up in two sentences: It was the best of teams. It was the worst of teams.

I confess I've dreamed of juxtaposing those two sentences. You might say it is a far far better paragraph than I have ever written.

As part of the pregame show on Fox, the network's sideline reporter, Ron Pitts, stood by the end-zone stands at Lambeau and, downplaying LeRoy Butler's seminal contribution, explained that on this spot Robert Brooks created the Leap. ("It's like you're a rock star," Brooks says, "and you trust your fans completely, and you dive off the stage.") Pitts was no stranger to Lambeau. He had been a defensive back for the Packers in the late 1980s, and twenty years earlier, he had watched his father, Elijah Pitts, replace Paul Hornung in the Green Bay backfield. Elijah Pitts ran for two touchdowns in Super Bowl I. Many of the old Packers have had sons who played high school or college football, and one, Jim Flanigan, has a son who plays for the Chicago Bears, but Ron Pitts is, so far, the only second-generation Packer.

*   *   *

A "gray" ghost mingled with the Lambeau crowd for the Carolina game: Tony Canadeo, a member of the Packers' Board of Directors and of the Pro Football Hall of Fame. In 1949, Canadeo ran for more than 1,000 yards, the third player in NFL history to reach that mark. He was known as "The Grey Ghost of Gonzaga," a tribute to his hair color, his elusiveness, and his alma mater. Even though Canadeo's name may no longer be familiar to younger fans, he is probably still the third most famous person ever to come out of Gonzaga University. John Stockton, the basketball player, might win the votes of most younger fans, but Stockton would have to settle for second place, far behind the singer Bing Crosby.

Canadeo's fellow director, Willie Davis, paid a quick visit to the Green Bay locker room, the only old Packer to invade the sanctuary before the game. "Play big," he urged Reggie White and his defensive teammates. "This is the day you step up."

The young Packers nodded.

Boyd Dowler scored the first two touchdowns in the Ice Bowl, both on passes from Starr, the first for 8 yards, the second for 43, staking the Packers to a 14–0 lead in the first half. The second touchdown came on third-and-one at the Dallas 43-yard line, a bold strike, a trademark passing play for Starr and Dowler and Lombardi.

In 1996, when the Chicago Bears came to Lambeau Field, Dowler served as honorary captain and applauded a Green Bay victory. But a month later, as he sat down to watch the NFC championship game in his home in Tampa, Florida, Boyd Dowler was rooting for the Carolina Panthers.

"I'm a scout for the Panthers," Dowler explained. "They pay my salary."

Dowler laughed. "But if the Packers should upset the mighty Panthers, I'll root for them in the Super Bowl."

Actually, the Packers were favored to beat the Panthers, favored by twelve-and-a-half points. Holmgren, faithful to the coaching code, protested that his team didn't deserve to be favored by that much. But the truth was, the Packers did deserve to be heavy favorites.

The Packers had a 13–3 regular-season record, the best in the National Conference. They had scored more points than any other team in the NFL, and had allowed fewer. They had tied the Green Bay record for victories, set by Lombardi's 1962 Packers. They had won eight games by twenty or more points, matching an arcane NFL record set by the Frankford Yellow Jackets in 1924. They had won their last six games, including a divisional playoff game, running away with the final four by an average score of 36–8.

Carolina, on paper, was no pushover. The Panthers had won eight straight games, had defeated San Francisco twice during the regular season, and only a week earlier had stopped Dallas, the reigning Super Bowl champion, to reach the NFC title game. The Panthers had a 13–4 record, including the playoff victory against the Cowboys. Their defense, rattling enemy quarterbacks with its zone blitz, had registered a league-high 60 sacks and permitted only 56 points in the second half of sixteen regular-season games, fewer than 4 points a half, an NFL record. Three of their linebackers had been selected for the Pro Bowl.

During the Packers' first full workout to get ready for Carolina, the Wednesday before the game, Holmgren had been uncommonly tense. He'd acted as if the Packers were preparing to play the 1972 Dolphins or the 1985 Bears, instead of the 1996 Panthers. "I was yelling at everybody," he says. He screamed at Favre when Brett, facing a simulated Panther rush, and confused at first by the zone blitz, threw a few interceptions. Holmgren screamed at the defense, too. "I was going after them pretty good," he says. "I was pretty fired up."

After the practice session, Reggie White called a team meeting, players only, and after that meeting, the coach gave the minister a pep talk. "You've waited your whole life for this game," Holmgren said.

"I know this is the biggest game of my life," White said.

"Okay, you've been talking about it forever," Holmgren said. "Now do it."

White nodded. "Want me to tell you what the team meeting was about?" he asked.

"No, not really," Holmgren said. "That's your business."

"I'll tell you anyway," Reggie said. "I told the younger guys not to worry about you, that you'd settle down and be okay for the game."

On videotape, the Panthers did not particularly frighten the Packers. The offensive unit figured it could adjust to, and blunt, the zone blitz, and the defense was supremely confident. "When we talked among ourselves," Eugene Robinson said, "the feeling was, 'Hey, this team can't beat us. I don't care how you slice it, this team cannot win.' "

(The Super Bowl I Packers had reacted similarly to films of their opponents, the Kansas City Chiefs: "Looks like Looney Tunes and Merrie Melodies," said Max McGee after watching two Kansas City defensive backs collide. The Super Bowl III New York Jets, preparing for the Baltimore Colts, had fun at the flicks, too. "Damn, Joe, we better stop watching those movies," a teammate told Joe Namath, "or we're gonna get overconfident.")

The Panthers, a second-year expansion team built around veteran players, were playing only the thirty-fourth game of their existence. No expansion team had ever achieved so much so quickly. But the Panthers' thirty-fourth game was the first they had played in Lambeau Field, and not only the ghosts were out to get them. So was the weather.

The weather was officially listed as cold and windy, and the temperature at game time was 3 degrees above zero, driven down to −17 by the wind-chill factor. Carolina had never in its brief history played a game when the temperature was below 34 degrees. Brett Favre had never lost a home game when the temperature dipped to 34 or lower; he was 18–0 on the frozen fields of Wisconsin. But he still didn't *like* Jack Frost nipping at his toes . "I can't stand the cold," the young Mississippian said a few days before the Carolina game. "I absolutely hate it." His backup, Jim McMahon, Favre explained, felt differently. "McMahon loves it," Favre said. "He's kind of numb to everything."

The Packers' edge was more psychological than physical. The Packers themselves never practiced outdoors in subfreezing temperatures. They practiced indoors. But they lived in Green Bay, and if you live in Green Bay, you live with cold and, to an extent, you develop a tolerance for it. "We might have a little advantage," Favre conceded. "It's our turf, our tundra."

Thirteen below for the Ice Bowl.

It was the best of temps. It was the worst of temps.

It was the best because it was historic, the coldest setting ever for an NFL game. It was the worst because a generation of fans, and a generation of wary football players, grew up thinking that the temperature in Green Bay was always thirteen below.

Actually, three NFL games have been played at temperatures of zero or below, and the Ice Bowl was the only one of the three that was played in Green Bay.

"With Vince Lombardi," Fuzzy Thurston remembers, "it was never cold here. 'It's our kind of day,' he'd say. 'Now get out there and strut around like it's the middle of July.' "

* * *

Gilbert Brown, the massive defensive lineman, came out on the field to "warm up" in shorts. He made certain the Carolina Panthers saw his bare and beefy legs. Lombardi would have loved him.

Never before had a football game been played in Green Bay so deep into winter as January 12. The record low for a January 12 in the city was 25 below, set in 1912, before the NFL was born. The record snow for a January 12 was eleven-and-a-half inches.

Three above, and sunny, was almost tropical.

"This is too nice a day," Paul Hornung, a guest on the pregame show, told the WTMJ radio audience. "Let's have it a little bit more cool. No sun. About a fifteen-to-twenty-mile-an-hour wind blowing."

Hornung chuckled. "The people in these stands," he said, "will remember being here at Lambeau more than any other game if the Packers win. They'll say, 'Boy, was it cold, but we didn't give a damn how cold it was.' This is a special game. This is the way the game is supposed to be played. Outside. Cold as hell. January. This is where it's at."

Then Hornung bundled up in a fur coat to participate in the pregame ceremonies on the playing field.

Willie Davis shivered as he came out of the Packers' locker room. "How in hell did we ever play a game in weather like this?" said Davis, who now lives in the warmth of Los Angeles.

* * *

The twenty thousand programs printed for the Carolina game were sold out at $6 apiece ninety minutes before the kickoff. Packer City Antiques, a local shop, sold twenty-five programs the following day for $20 to $25 apiece. The programs became antiques overnight.

On his way into the stadium, Greg Schwister lost his wallet, which contained sixty dollars and his prized ticket. He was devastated, until he went to the police, who informed him that another fan, Darryl Ruprecht of Green Bay, had turned in the wallet, the money, and the ticket, all intact.

Mike Holmgren delivered a variation on his standard pregame speech. He reminded his players of the importance of the moment, reminded them how hard they had worked to reach the NFC championship, how much they had to gain, how much they had to lose. He mentioned that this was a special opportunity that some of them would never have again. Then Holmgren left the room and turned the team over to one of its newest members, the wide receiver, Andre Previn Rison. (Wouldn't you think that if Rison's mother was going to name him after one of Mia Farrow's former husbands, she would have called him Frank Sinatra Rison?)

Rison came to the Packers with a reputation for a burgeoning ego and a diminishing talent. He had been selected in the first round of the 1989 draft by the Indianapolis Colts, who, after his solid rookie season, traded Rison to the Atlanta Falcons. He put in five impressive seasons in Atlanta, caught more than eighty passes each year, was chosen four times for the Pro Bowl and once was the game's Most Valuable Player. Andre was compared to Jerry Rice, often favorably and often by himself, but he couldn't understand why he was called cocky, arrogant, and flamboyant. "I am one of the nicest people you'd ever want to meet," he explained. His girlfriend, Lisa "Left Eye" Lopez, one-third of the singing group TLC, burned down his Atlanta mansion after a spat. He later married her.

His closest friend on the Falcons was Deion Sanders, the two of them sharing the spotlight on a team that produced only one winning season despite the presence of two self-confessed superstars. "God, it was frustrating," Rison told me, soon after he became a Packer, "seeing all those other guys who you thought you were better than, being in the right place at the right time, playing on championship-caliber teams.

"We thought maybe we could do it in Atlanta, but then Deion got the opportunity to go play in San Francisco, and I felt happy for him, but I was mad, too, 'cause that was my partner leaving, and we were losing probably the best cornerback ever to play the game.

"And you could see his play just went up two or three notches in San Francisco, because he felt good putting on that uniform, looking around the locker room, and seeing that everyone in there was a winner.

"When he got that first ring, I didn't want to see it.

I told him I didn't want to see it. I didn't want to see a Super Bowl ring till I put one on my finger."

In 1995, as a free agent, Rison considered the Green Bay Packers, but signed with the Cleveland Browns, and his pass-catching totals, and his stock, both plummeted. When the Browns abandoned Cleveland for Baltimore, they abandoned Rison, too. He signed with the Jacksonville Jaguars, the expansion team, but halfway through the 1996 season—"I thought I was playing great, but they thought otherwise"—the Jaguars gave up on him and released him.

On November 18, the day he became unemployed, Rison went to a party in New York to celebrate the release of a new album featuring duets by singing stars and NFL stars. During the party, the Monday Night Football game between Dallas and Green Bay unfolded on a giant screen. Rison watched. He stood next to Robert Brooks, one of three Green Bay receivers (Antonio Freeman and Mark Chmura were the other two), all starters at the beginning of the season, who had been sidelined by injuries.

The Packers fizzled offensively against Dallas. Favre floundered. "Man, we could use you," Brooks said to Rison. "We could use you tonight."

Rison agreed. "Yeah," he said. "I wish I was there tonight."

A few hours later, on an unhappy plane ride home from Dallas to Green Bay, Mike Holmgren and Ron Wolf talked about their team's sagging passing attack. They knew they badly needed a new receiver. They decided they would try to sign Andre Rison. Holmgren knew Andre from the Pro Bowl. Holmgren's offensive coordinator, Sherman Lewis, knew him from Michigan State, their mutual alma mater. They both knew him from flirting with him in 1995. They sensed, *hoped*, that he would not be a disruptive influence, that he would fit in with the Packers. "We were desperate," Holmgren says.

Rison said San Francisco and Kansas City were also interested in him, and probably Hollywood and Madison Avenue, too, but he leaped for the Packers' offer. He agreed to terms the day after the Dallas game, and the next day walked into Holmgren's office. "Nothing that happened before you walked through that door exists," Holmgren said. "You're a Packer now."

Rison was ecstatic. "The tradition of this organization automatically makes you appreciate the opportunity," he said. "Bart Starr. Vince Lombardi. The Packer tradition almost transcends football."

He was off to a good start. He had gone a whole paragraph without mentioning himself.

Rison did well on the field, too. He started four of the Packers' last five games and caught his share of passes, two or three most games, five one game. He did not demand the ball. He did not demand to be the star. When Antonio Freeman reentered the lineup, Rison functioned primarily as a decoy, drawing double coverage. "I don't think enough can be said about the unselfish play of Andre Rison," Freeman said. "Here's a guy that's accustomed to getting the ball five to ten times a game. It's not happening here. He's doing a great job of drawing the defense away from me and making it very easy for me to get open." The first two times he teamed with Rison, Freeman enjoyed the two best games of his career, ten catches against Chicago and nine against Denver, for a total of 331 yards.

"We haven't thrown Andre the ball enough," Holmgren said late in the regular season. "It's my job to make sure Andre touches the ball more. I just want to make sure he understands he is helping us even if he isn't getting the ball."

Holmgren made the statement to reporters, but aimed it at Rison. The first two sentences, the coach meant, sort of. The third sentence, he meant, absolutely. Holmgren was, as usual, selling selflessness, emphasizing the team over the individual. The Packers heard the message, and bought it. One of their favorite locker-room phrases was, "Super Bowl before Pro Bowl." Next to "Shit be bringin' it, hoss," of course.

LeRoy Butler convinced Holmgren to allow Rison to address the team before the Carolina game. Rison started off calmly, thanking his teammates for accepting him, for allowing him to become a part of their family. He told them how much he had grown to love them. Then Rison turned combative.

Michael Silver in *Sports Illustrated* said LeRoy Butler called Rison's speech "hip-hop Lombardi," which is a pretty slick phrase for a defensive back, or anyone else. But, since Butler has been known to refer to "social Darwinism," in discussing his adjustment to Green Bay, I'll give him "hip-hop Lombardi," too.

By any name, Rison's words were a blend of motivation and attitude, spiced with obscenity. "I wasn't here for the Dallas game last year, but I hear a lot of y'all talk about the bitter taste it left in your mouths," Rison said, according to Silver's sources. "Well, fuck that taste. This isn't the Super Bowl—it's bigger. There's no way we can let the media intimidate us, telling our offense how it has to handle the zone blitz. The hell with that. They've got to stop us. We've got too many weapons. So let's go out there, run our offense, and kick their ass."

Some of his teammates remember Rison ending by calling Lambeau Field "our house"—his old friend Deion used to refer to the Georgia Dome, with less modesty, as "my house"—and insisting, "Nobody is coming into our fucking house and beating us."

Modified Lombardi or modified Deion, Rison's speech had an impact. "Everyone got chills," the tight end, Jeff Thomason, says. "We were fired up after that."

Mike Holmgren is a big man, a bulky six-foot-five with a mustache that makes him look like a walrus. He has no airs, no pretense to him, displays little of the paranoia that afflicts too many coaches and, unless you play for him and commit stupidity, he is not intimidating. Unlike Lombardi, he does not set out to strike fear into players and reporters. Like Lombardi, his knowledge and his work ethic command respect.

Holmgren was raised in San Francisco, a high school and college quarterback in the sixties, when Lombardi's teams bestrode the NFL. Holmgren was a 49ers fan, but he was also a Bart Starr fan, and he knew very well the names of Starr's Green Bay teammates. Once, on a Friday night, when he was a teenager, he was cruising North Beach with a group of his high-school buddies, and as they passed Pierre's, a popular watering hole, Holmgren looked inside and did a double-take. "Holy shit," he said, "there's Jimmy Taylor!"

Holmgren looked again. "Holy shit," he added. "He's shit faced!"

In fairness to Taylor, Jimmy never did drink as well as he ran. A couple of beers sufficed to turn him shit faced. Max McGee recalls a time in San Francisco, possibly even the same night, when he and Hornung informed Taylor, who had downed a beer or two, that a young woman sitting at the bar was showing great interest in him. They pointed to a mannequin someone had propped up on a bar stool. Taylor walked up to the mannequin and asked her how she was doing. It could've been worse. Joe Namath once had a similar experience with a female impersonator.

Holmgren, who was good enough in high school to start opposite the future Heisman Trophy winner, Jim Plunkett, in a California all-star game, then played college football at the University of Southern California. In his junior year with the Trojans, his main function was to hand the ball off to a running back named O. J. Simpson. In those days, O.J. *was* the West Coast offense. One of the quarterbacks who had preceded Holmgren at USC was Willie Wood.

The links between the Packers of the sixties and the Packers of the nineties are endless. One of Wood's backfield coaches at USC was Al Davis, who later, as the owner of the Oakland Raiders, hired and trained Ron Wolf. Another of Wood's backfield coaches at USC was John McKay, who later, as head coach of the Trojans, recruited and tutored Mike Holmgren.

In January 1967, the first "Super Bowl" game—it was not yet officially called the Super Bowl, but more formally the AFL-NFL World Championship Game—was played in the Los Angeles Coliseum, on the home field of the USC Trojans. The tickets cost $6 and $12, and more than 30,000, of roughly 94,000, went unsold. Because the game was not a sellout, the television coverage was blacked out in the Los Angeles area.

Mike Holmgren probably could have talked his way into the stadium without paying. He might even have been able to come up with the money for a ticket. But he had a friend who lived in the San Fernando Valley and who insisted he had figured out a way to bootleg the television pictures of the game. Holmgren went to his friend's home for the game and, of course, they weren't able to get a picture. The Packers' future coach did not see the Packers win Super Bowl I. He did not see Willie Wood, his fellow Trojan, return an interception 50 yards to break open a close game in the third quarter.

Wood himself later became a head coach in both the World Football League and the Canadian. He knows the game. "I talk to Mike whenever I come to Green Bay," Wood said. "Mostly, I just compliment him and his assistants, tell them I appreciate what they're doing, and then stay out of their way."

*   *   *

A Country and Western singer named Toby Keith sang "The Star Spangled Banner" before the Packers played Carolina. Nobody was quite sure why. Several years earlier, Keith had written a country hit, "Should've Been a Cowboy." Perhaps he was chosen to symbolize the Packers' disappointment. They had been looking forward to playing the Cowboys in Lambeau. They had been looking forward to revenge. They had lost eight straight games to the Cowboys, the last seven in Dallas. They were hoping to get even on their own field.

The field was in surprisingly good condition. It had been devastated the previous week, strafed by rain and ice, so muddied and chewed up that the NFL decided, at an expense of more than $100,000, to bring in 85,000 cubic feet of fresh sod from Duro-Turf, a sod farm in Maryland. Twenty-eight heated tractor-trailers moved the earth to Wisconsin, and, with groundskeepers Chip Toma of the NFL and Todd Edlebeck of the Packers supervising the installation, the entire field was replaced in two days.

The old sod was broken up into squares, 5 inches by 5 inches, which were placed in 25,000 boxes, then sold for $10 a box. Every box was purchased within two hours, and the proceeds were divided among four local charities: The Freedom House Homeless Shelter, the Family Violence Center, the Curative Rehabilitation Center, and a sports booster group at the University of Wisconsin–Green Bay. The boxes, in green and gold, were marked "Frozen Tundra," which is catchy, but redundant. Tundra, by definition, *is* frozen: "Black mucky soil with a permanently frozen subsoil," *Webster's* informs.

Mike Holmgren wished his Packers were not playing the Carolina Panthers in the NFC championship game. He wished they were playing the Dallas Cowboys, even though he believed the Cowboys were a better team than the Panthers. "It was probably silly," Holmgren says, "but I'd be lying if I didn't say I wanted to get the Cowboys in Lambeau."

Silly, illogical, or irrational, many of Holmgren's players, not all, shared their coach's feeling. They wanted to show they could beat the team they had never beaten. They told themselves they could beat the Cowboys in Green Bay. They watched the Dallas-Carolina game and, uncomfortably, rooted for the Cowboys.

When Carolina won, Holmgren feared that his players might not take the Panthers as seriously as they took the Cowboys, worried that they might be less motivated. Of course he did not tell his players any of this. He told them that the Panthers were the best team in the world.

There was also the danger that the players, the coaches, the entire organization was looking past the Panthers to the Super Bowl. During the week before the NFC championship game, I heard Green Bay executives talking about where the team would be staying in New Orleans, where they would be practicing, how and when they would be getting their Super Bowl tickets.

And they weren't saying "if;" they were saying "when." I wondered if the Carolina people were having the same confident conversations.

"Are you re-a-a-a-d-y?" Gary Knafelc boomed on the P.A., and then, almost lost in an explosion of cheers, he introduced the starting offensive lineup for the home team. Favre, as always, got the loudest ovation. He was starting his eighty-sixth straight game; no other quarterback in the NFL had a streak even half as long.

Traditionally, quarterbacks, the highest paid and hardest hit of professional players, buy expensive gifts for their offensive linemen, rewards for keeping the quarterbacks intact. Once, steak dinners were considered adequate and appropriate, but the price of protection has gone up considerably in recent years, and now Rolex watches, trips to Hawaii, and state-of-the-art hunting and fishing gear are not uncommon. Favre's linemen love to call him the cheapest quarterback in the NFL, but during the 1996 season he risked his image by investing in new suits for his blockers. He brought a tailor to the locker room to measure the 300-pounders. A rookie guard, Marco Rivera, who spent the entire season on the roster, but never dressed for a game, was all excited. "I don't even own a suit," he said. He does now.

Favre's backup, Jim McMahon, threw four passes all year, completed three of them. His quarterback rating of 105.9 would have been the best in the NFL if he had thrown only 220 more passes. He did not buy gifts for the offensive line because he rarely saw those men from the back. But McMahon performed a much rarer generous deed. On at least two occasions, he paid to have steak and lobsters flown in, cooked and served to all the Packers' trainers, maintenance workers, and equipment men.

A few minutes before kickoff time, Hornung and Wood, the honorary co-captains, walked to the center of the field, escorted by the Packers' six active captains, Reggie White and LeRoy Butler representing the defense, Brett Favre and Frank Winters the offense, and Mike Prior and Desmond Howard the special teams. Favre turned to Hornung and Wood and said, "Really appreciate you guys being here." Butler said he felt chills seeing Hornung, who still held the NFL record for points scored in a season, 176 in 1960, a *twelve-game* season. "Awesome," said Butler, who had, on occasion, discussed the intricacies of playing defensive back with Herb Adderley and Willie Wood.

Wood and Desmond Howard had met previously at golf outings in Washington, D.C., Wood's hometown. Howard, the 1991 Heisman Trophy winner at Michigan, the fourth player chosen in the 1992 draft, had spent his first three seasons, less than spectacularly, with the Redskins. Wood told Howard how pleased people in Washington were with Desmond's achievements in Green Bay in 1996. "You don't realize how young these guys are till you get next to 'em," Wood said. "Desmond's an exciting little kid."

*   *   *

In 1961, Willie Wood was an exciting little kid, too, twenty-four years old, five-foot-ten, 180 pounds, exactly Howard's size. In his second NFL season, Wood averaged sixteen yards a punt return and returned two for touchdowns. In 1996, his first Packer season, Howard averaged fifteen yards a punt return and returned three for touchdowns. In between, no other Packer punt returner posted such impressive statistics.

The Panthers sent out honorary co-captains, too, their owner, Jerry Richardson, once a journeyman receiver for the Baltimore Colts, and their president, Mike McCormack, a Hall of Fame tackle for the Cleveland Browns. Both men had played against Lombardi's Packers, and McCormack had served as an assistant coach under Lombardi in Washington in 1969. In the 1970s, when McCormack was head coach of the Philadelphia Eagles, his secretary was a woman named Angela Cerelli, who left the Eagles to marry Paul Hornung. Football is a very small world.

Hornung and Wood had both been honorary captains in 1992, the first year of the practice, Hornung for a game in Green Bay against the Bears, the Packers' ancient rivals, the team Hornung most loved to hate. "I've been a cool, cocky character all my life," he says, "but when I came back as honorary captain for that Bears game, when they introduced me, they gave me a ten-minute standing ovation, and I shivered."

Maybe it wasn't quite *ten* minutes. Hornung has always had a weakness for hyperbole. "He makes a trip to the corner grocery sound like an Arctic expedition," my friend Jimmy Breslin, the Pulitzer Prize–winning columnist, once wrote.

Despite Hornung and Wood, the Packers lost the toss. Carolina chose to receive.

Ron Pitts, working the sidelines for Fox, managed to get in a last-minute on-camera question to Holmgren, pressing the coach to provide a clue to the outcome of the game. Holmgren, of course, replied by saying nothing, or next to it. "We can't turn the ball over," Holmgren said.

As Pitts moved away from Holmgren, out of camera range, he found himself next to Willie Wood, his father's former teammate. The two ex-Packers, ex-defensive backs and ex-punt returners hugged. "Willie used to tease me when I was a little kid," Pitts said, "and I loved it. It was the same feeling thirty years later. It was cold, and the crowd was making noise, and it was like I had never left. It was incredible."

Green Bay kicked off, and on the Panthers' first possession, they went nowhere. The Packers took over after a short punt, and on their first offensive play in the first championship game in their house in twenty-nine years, Favre hit Andre Rison for 8 yards.

"To pick up Rison when they did," Willie Davis said, "somebody that good at the right moment, they're a team of destiny."

The Packers drove for back-to-back first downs, each time, on third-and-one, Favre calling and executing a quarterback sneak to get the needed yard, awakening memories, again, of the Ice Bowl. The quarterback sneak on third-and-one had been a significant part of that game, too.

The offensive line in front of Favre—Bruce Wilkerson, Aaron Taylor, Frank Winters, Adam Timmerman, and Earl Dotson—*averaged* 303 pounds a man. The offensive line in front of Bart Starr three decades earlier—Bob Skoronski, Fuzzy Thurston, Ken Bowman, Jerry Kramer, and Forrest Gregg—averaged 244 pounds a man, a difference of fifty-nine pounds a man. Jerry Kramer looked at the young Packers and said, "Where's the valve? Where do you pump 'em up?"

On the roster for the Ice Bowl, not a single Packer was listed at more than 260 pounds. Ten were listed at six-foot-four or taller.

On the roster for the Carolina game, ten Packers were listed at more than 300 pounds. Sixteen were listed at six-foot-four or taller.

The 1996 Packers were heavier, taller, stronger, quicker, and, certainly not least, richer. Reggie White earned $4.5 million for the 1996 season, which was far more than double what Vince Lombardi paid all forty of his Super Bowl I Packers for the 1966 season.

Some things, however, were familiar. Just as several of Lombardi's Packers emerged from such underexposed collegiate football programs as Philander Smith, Arkansas A.M.&N., Valparaiso, Los Angeles State, and

Arlington State, some of Holmgren's Packers repre-
sented such lesser known schools as Chadron State,
Ball State, Gardner-Webb, Western Illinois, and South
Dakota State.

And, just as Willie Davis and Bart Starr and Marv
Fleming were late-round draft choices in their day,
Mark Chmura, Adam Timmerman, and Dorsey Levens
were tapped near the bottom of their drafts. Moreover,
each team had a free agent starting at free safety. No
one had drafted either Willie Wood, a Hall of Famer,
or Eugene Robinson, a Pro Bowler. Both came out of
college undersized and underrated, Wood from USC
and Robinson from Colgate; no one had been able to
measure what was inside them.

No school had more players on the 1966 or the 1996
rosters than Notre Dame. Guards Aaron Taylor and
Lindsay Knapp, punter Craig Hentrich, receiver Derrick
Mayes and running back Dorsey Levens, who transferred and finished his college career at Georgia Tech,
were Green Bay's "Irish" heirs to Paul Hornung and
Red Mack. Only fitting for a team that was founded by
a Notre Dame man.

Green Bay's first drive stalled at the Carolina 32-yard line
and, after an exchange of punts, the Packers were backed up
to their own 6-yard line. On second down, Favre, pressured by
the Panthers' zone blitz, tossed a pass right into the hands of
Sam Mills, one of Carolina's three Pro Bowl linebackers, a
first-time Pro Bowl starter at the late-blooming age of thirty-

seven. Mills returned the interception to the 2-yard line, setting up a touchdown and a quick 7–0 Carolina lead.

Sam Mills was the first player from his school, Montclair State University, to play in the NFL. Yet he was neither Montclair State's most accomplished athlete nor its most famous student, trailing Carol Blazejowski, who once scored a record 55 points in a basketball game in Madision Square Garden, in the former category, and Bruce Willis, the actor, in the latter.

John Madden, broadcasting the game on the Fox Sports Network, could not have been more delighted if he were sitting down to a side of beef in his private bus. "This is what it's all about!" Madden enthused. He loved football in Lambeau Field, in freezing weather, on real grass. He loved the legends, the tradition, the ghosts. Madden had made certain to pay a visit to Lombardi's old Green Bay home during the week leading up to the Carolina game. Madden and his broadcasting partner, Pat Summerall, both had lost to Lombardi's Packers in championship games, Madden when he was an assistant coach with the Oakland Raiders, Summerall when he was a player with the New York Giants.

In the living room of his home in Akron, Ohio, Dave Robinson, who played next to Nitschke in the sixties, camped in front of his television set, watching and taping the NFC championship game. "I'd told everybody

I was going out of town," Robby says. "I turned off the telephone. I didn't want any interruptions."

When Carolina jumped in front, Robinson got so anxious he couldn't sit still. He went into the kitchen and began peeling potatoes. "I had to do something," he says. "I couldn't just sit in front of the screen. It was too intense."

Robinson didn't return to the living room until he had prepared the entire Sunday dinner for his family. "Leg of lamb, mashed potatoes, gravy, the whole nine yards," he says. "Actually, I roasted two legs of lamb. My wife likes it well done and I like it rare. I kept sneaking peeks at the game on the kitchen TV and I got so excited both legs of lamb turned out well done."

When Robinson watched the game, he watched with the eye of a linebacker. *They'd never do that against Nitschke*, he thought. "I'm just prone to watch the defense," he says. "I live and die with the defense."

Of the Packers' defenders, the one Robby knows best, and admires most, is Reggie, with whom he shares a bond beyond football. Dave's late brother Frank was, like White, a minister. "We talk mostly about religion," Robinson says, "and about our families."

Early in the season, on Alumni Weekend, Robinson attended the San Diego game at Lambeau. "To me," he says, "it's still the hallowed field. When I walk on that field, I really want to put the pads on. I still got a couple hits left in me." Robby laughs. "I just can't *get* hit," he admits. "One hit from somebody, and I'm done."

Do any of the young Packer linebackers remind him of himself?

Robinson giggles again. "They're all too young, too smart and too fast," he says. "We played a different type of football than they do today. The linebackers of today are blitzers and sackers. We were interceptors. We were primarily pass-defense people. My allegiance was split between helping Willie Davis on the run and providing underneath coverage for Herb Adderley on the pass. It's all different now."

Not quite everything has changed. "We're all Green Bay Packers," Robinson says. "We all have green-and-gold blood."

Ray Nitschke snarled instructions from the private box he was sharing with a group that included Paul Tagliabue, the commissioner of the National Football League, and three of Ray's former teammates, Bart Starr, Willie Davis, and Jerry Kramer. "Hey, man," Nitschke shouted, "that guy's holding the ball like a loaf of bread!"

Nitschke wished he could grab the loaf of bread. "Sometimes it hurts to watch," he says. "You want to be out there. But you know you can't be."

Nitschke watched as fan and reporter. He writes a weekly column in the *Packer Report*, which is to Green Bay football what *Variety* is to show business. He is called a "featured columnist." In the issue before the Carolina game, Nitschke began his featured column, on the victory over San Francisco, "This game showed the Green Bay Packers are for real." Nitschke writes better than I tackle, but not a whole lot.

*   *   *

In retrospect, the Packers' 1996 season, their regular season, can be divided into three separate installments: A superb start and a matching finish, sandwiched around a troubling slump. In the beginning, the Packers were invincible. They won the first three games on their schedule for the first time in thirty years, for the first time since the Super Bowl I team.

And they won their first three games far more convincingly than the 1966 Packers did. They outscored their opponents, 115–26; their average margin of victory was better than four touchdowns. They scored 65 points (to 13) in the first half and they never trailed, not for a second, not by a point. The individual statistics were equally impressive:

Brett Favre, storming back from rehab, threw ten touchdown passes and only one interception; "I told you guys, 'Don't bet against me,' " he reminded reporters.

Robert Brooks caught sixteen passes, scored two touchdowns and earned perfect 10s for his two Lambeau Leaps; he also soared to the top of the music charts in Wisconsin with his hit single, "Jump (in the Stands)," which he wrote, arranged, performed, produced, mixed, and plugged.

Keith Jackson, who didn't re-sign with the Packers till July, scored four touchdowns; he had seriously considered leaving Green Bay to sign with New Orleans, or leaving football to accept a television offer.

LeRoy Butler intercepted four passes and returned one 90 yards for a touchdown, setting up the second

Lambeau Leap of his career; this time, the man who invented the Leap reached the seats, with a helping hand from the fans.

Reggie White was credited with 2½ sacks, raising his career total to 159½, far ahead of any other player in NFL history.

At halftime of the third straight one-sided victory, the Packers honored the men who had played in Super Bowl I and II, prompting Mike Holmgren to be asked if the present team measured up to the past.

"That would be very flattering," Coach Holmgren said, "but I have always said that that group of men and Coach Lombardi and that era will never be duplicated. Now if we can *approach* some of that, at some point, great."

The Packers lost their next game. They lost to the Minnesota Vikings in the Metrodome for the fifth year in a row. They lost for the twelfth time in thirteen games on artificial turf.

When Lombardi used to get angry at his Packers, he would tell them that they couldn't beat The Little Sisters of the Poor.

The Packers still couldn't. Not on artificial turf under a dome.

The Seattle Seahawks were no Little Sisters of the Poor. The Packers beat them the next week, on artificial turf in the Kingdome, the start of a five-game winning streak. The first two were blowouts. The next was a war: Down by 11 points at halftime, down by three points with ten seconds to go, the Packers rallied and, on Chris Jacke's 53-yard field goal, beat the San Francisco 49ers in overtime. They won the war, but lost a star. Robert Brooks ripped up his right knee on the first offensive play of the game. Their best receiver, best Leaper, and best vocalist was out for the season. Don Beebe came in and caught eleven passes for 220 yards against the 49ers, the biggest game of his career. But his singing was dreadful.

Brooks's injury, in their seventh game, was the Packers' first significant injury of the season, a major factor in their strong start. The same eleven men had started the first seven games for the Packers on defense; nine men had started the first seven games on offense. The only changes, at left tackle and at fullback, were for tactical reasons, not medical.

The Packers struggled, but survived the first two weeks without Brooks. They barely beat Tampa Bay and lost Antonio Freeman with a broken left forearm. They came from behind to beat Detroit and almost lost Don Beebe. He took a pair of hits that looked as if they would have leveled leviathans. Beebe is five-foot-eleven and 183 pounds. The first blow knocked the breath out of him; the second knocked the sense out of him. Beebe got his breath back, and his brain, then teamed up with Favre on a 65-yard touchdown pass.

Susan Lombardi, the coach's daughter, participated in a pregame ceremony introducing the artwork for a Vince Lombardi postage stamp, part of a series, to be released in 1997, honoring legendary coaches. On the stamp, Lombardi was smiling.

So were the Packers. They were 8–1, their best start since Lombardi's 1963 team.

They had forced the opposition into twenty-nine turnovers in nine games; they had caused only sixteen turnovers the whole previous season.

Brett Favre's efficiency rating was 99.9; no other quarterback in the league was above 90.

Everyone was talking Super Bowl for the Packers.

Everyone except Mike Holmgren. He told his players not to say "Super Bowl" out loud or he would kill them.

The Packers' receivers were clearly a talented, if brittle, group.

In the spring of 1987, as Don Beebe approached his twenty-third birthday, he had never played one down of college football. Ten years later, he had played on five Super Bowl teams. That is, at least, a small miracle. Beebe insists it is a holy miracle.

He had, in his teens, briefly enrolled in two separate colleges, Western Illinois and Aurora, and quickly decided that college was not for him. He had spent the next three years working on a constuction job, keeping in terrific shape. Then, Beebe says, "I felt the Lord wanted me to go back into football." He re-enrolled at Western Illinois, which figured out that, because of his age and his academic history, he was entitled to only one year of football eligibility.

One day during spring practice in 1987, Beebe happened to walk through the gym as a group of NFL scouts were sizing up a few Western Illinois seniors, including the team's most valuable player, the center, Frank Winters. The seniors were running 40-yard dashes.

"Can I run?" Beebe asked.

He was wearing a tank top, shorts, and sandals. His sneakers were in his dorm room.

The Western Illinois coach suggested that Beebe not waste the scouts' time.

"I really want to run," Beebe insisted.

"Let the kid run," said one of the scouts, who represented the Dallas Cowboys.

Beebe took off his sandals, ran barefoot, and ran the fastest 40 ever timed in the Western Illinois gym, a fraction over 4.3 seconds.

"Son, come here," the Dallas scout said. "What's your name?"

"Don Beebe."

"What number are you on the films?"

"I'm not in the films," Beebe said. "I haven't played a game yet. I have one year of eligibility left."

The scout could hardly believe Beebe. "You just ran a four-three-something forty, and you've never . . ." The scout shook his head. "We'll be watching you."

Beebe played one season for Western Illinois, then discovered that he still had another season of eligibility not at the NCAA level, but at the NAIA, an organization of generally smaller and more flexible schools. Illinois Benedictine College, close to his home in Aurora, pursued Beebe, but he visited the campus and decided, "This isn't where the Lord wants me to be."

Then he got a phone call from a former Western

Illinois coach who had switched to Chadron State.

"Chadron what?" said Beebe.

"Chadron State. It's in Nebraska. Get out your map."

Beebe took out a map, looked around Omaha, looked around Lincoln, the only cities he'd heard of in Nebraska, and saw no Chadron. "Look in the north-west corner, south of the Black Hills."

Beebe found Chadron, close to South Dakota, and in the fall of 1988, he and Diana, his new bride, arrived with a U-Haul, one hundred dollars to their name, no place to live, and no imminent income. They spent the first night sleeping in their car in a parking lot. At six in the morning, they were awakened by a woman, a local resident, rapping on their window, wondering what they were doing in the lot. Within eight hours, the woman had found them a place to rent and a job for Diana.

Beebe played one season for Chadron, then im-pressed a scout who made a rare visit to the Nebraska campus. The scout got Beebe invited to the combine, the mass NFL tryout camp in Indianapolis, and Beebe's performance—the fastest forty of all the wide receivers, including blue-chip prospect Andre Rison—persuaded more than twenty scouts to flock to Chadron to inspect him more closely. He ran 4.21 for the New York Jets. He ran 4.28 for the Buffalo Bills, who drafted him in the third round.

Two years later, Buffalo went to its first Super Bowl.

The following year, Beebe scored his first Super Bowl touchdown.

And the year after that, he scored again and made

one of the most memorable plays in Super Bowl history, coming from 25 yards behind, catching up to Dallas's Leon Lett, who was running with a recovered fumble, and stripping him of the ball just as Lett thought he was going to prance into the end zone. Buffalo, by then, had no chance to win the game, but Beebe wouldn't quit.

"If it wasn't for my faith and the Lord opening doors for me," Beebe says, "I don't know where I'd be."

Beebe spent six seasons in Buffalo and one in Carolina before signing with Green Bay in 1996 at the age of thirty-one. "I thought Green Bay was about the same size as Buffalo, you know, a million people," Beebe says. "When I found out it was a hundred thousand, I said, 'No way.' But if you're a Packer player, you think there's four million and all of them are cheering for you. During training camp, thousands of people watched practice every day, and fifty thousand came to see a scrimmage."

Beyond the fans, what impressed Beebe most about his new team was the tolerance, the willingness to accept people for what they did on the football field, not to judge them by their religious beliefs or their racial background or their social habits; he also appreciated the lack of ego, the unselfishness, the absence of star complexes, and the courage of Brett Favre, his willingness to stand up to blitzing linebackers and to his own addiction. "Nine out of ten guys in this league would have hid in the closet and never brought the Vicodin up," Beebe says.

Beebe faced his own smaller crisis during the season.

His wife was due to give birth to their third child the weekend of the Kansas City game. Beebe told coach Holmgren that his family was his priority, that he intended to be with his wife during delivery even if he missed the game. Holmgren said he understood perfectly. Two days before the game, Diana elected to have labor induced. Beebe greeted his new daughter, kissed his wife, then flew off to Kansas City.

Beebe knew and accepted his role on the 1996 Packers, playing behind Robert Brooks and Antonio Freeman, then behind Andre Rison and Freeman, as he had played behind James Lofton and Andre Reed in Buffalo. "I have no problem with that role," he says. "And just as James Lofton taught me a lot, I can teach Antonio Freeman."

In the regular season, Beebe caught thirty-nine passes for 699 yards and four touchdowns, the most productive of his eight years in the NFL. For his eleven catches and 220 yards against San Francisco, he was named the NFL's Miller Lite Player of the Week.

Beebe, who grew up in Illinois loving the Bears and hating the Packers, received the award from Ray Nitschke at a press conference.

Beebe was born two years after Nitschke was named the Most Valuable Player in the 1962 NFL championship game.

So this is the great Ray Nitschke, Beebe thought, and was impressed.

Antonio Freeman grew up in Baltimore, in the heart of the inner city, surrounded by drugs and violence and broken families. "I lived with my mother and my father," Freeman says, "and I had an older brother who disciplined me and an older sister who went to college." A nuclear family was almost as rare in the neighborhood as a nuclear physicist. "They called us the Huxtables," Freeman recalls.

In high school, at Baltimore Poly, Freeman often ran a basic pass route, an "out" route which his coach called a "Carroll Dale." Freeman had no idea why the route was called a "Carroll Dale," no idea that Carroll Dale had been a wide receiver for Virginia Tech and the Green Bay Packers, no idea that he, too, would someday play for Virginia Tech and the Packers, no idea that, on November 3, 1996, Carroll Dale would be the honorary captain of the Packers. "Really weird," Freeman says.

Ironically, Freeman didn't get to meet Carroll Dale. Freeman didn't suit up on November 3. He was nursing the forearm he had fractured the previous week against Tampa Bay.

When Freeman came out of Virginia Tech, he expected to be drafted in the first two rounds. He wasn't picked until the third. "I feel as though God wanted me to be in Green Bay," Freeman says, "so He held me off."

In his first season as a Packer, Freeman contributed more as a punt and kickoff returner than as a pass receiver. He caught only eight passes all year, found the Packer passing attack more complicated and confusing than he had expected. He worked out at four different pass-catching positions.

"Flanker, you're normally the number one read," he says. "The split end seems to be the guy who occupies the defense and makes room for the flanker to come in and work. Then you have the three-wide-receiver set and the four-wide-receiver set. In this offensive system, you can change two words in the play call, and your assignment is completely different from what it was if you didn't change those two words. It's really hard to explain. It's extremely complex. It's mind-boggling. It's difficult for a young guy. Robert Brooks sat me down and explained it all to me."

Freeman caught on in 1996, his second season. He started the year at split end, switched to flanker when Brooks went down, switched back to split end after Andre Rison came in. In half the games he played, he caught six or more passes. He wound up with fifty-six receptions for 933 yards and nine touchdowns, better numbers than Carroll Dale posted in any of his thirteen seasons in the NFL.

Maybe they run an "Antonio Freeman" at Baltimore Poly now.

Except when Keith Jackson and Mark Chmura, a complementary couple of Pro Bowlers, were on the field at the same time, the Packers' fulltime tight end might as well have been called Keith Chmura or Mark Jackson. They were a perfect package between them, Jackson the more accomplished at catching passes, Chmura the more accomplished at blocking people.

Jackson had an uncanny nose for the end zone. Of the first eleven passes he caught in 1996, six were for

touchdowns; he finished the year with ten touchdowns, tying Dorsey Levens for the team lead.

Chmura had an uncanny nose for hitting people, for
"blowing people up," as the Packers liked to say. He
didn't score a touchdown all year; he opened holes for
others to score.

Jackson and Chmura, dividing playing time, could
easily have had a competitive, even antagonistic relationship. After all, Jackson, in his ninth NFL season,
twice All-Pro and five times selected for the Pro Bowl,
had always been a starter till he came to Green Bay,
reluctantly reporting six games into the 1995 season.

Reggie White used his most persuasive powers to get
Jackson, who shared Reggie's zest for religion and thirst
for a Super Bowl ring, to sign in 1995 and re-sign in
1996. "Reggie wanted someone to be with him spiri-
tually and mentally," Jackson says. Reggie, who also
urged Sean Jones and Eugene Robinson to become
Packers ("He said he was praying for me," Robinson
recalls), may be the greatest recruiter in the state of
Wisconsin since Al McGuire stopped persuading inner-
city kids to play basketball at Marquette.

In Green Bay, Jackson became Chmura's backup.
But, instead of sulking or gloating, Jackson and
Chmura recognized and respected each other's talents.
Typically, when the Detroit Lions came to Green Bay
midway through the 1996 season and the Packer
coaching staff devised a play in which the tight end
was the primary receiver, Chmura and Jackson agreed
that the play was better suited to Keith's skills. When

Favre called the play, Chmura, who was on the field, motioned to Jackson to replace him and ran toward the bench. Jackson came in and made the catch, setting up a Packer touchdown.

"You don't see a lot of jealousy in our locker room," Keith Jackson says. "You see a lot of love."

Robert Brooks could have been resentful, too, could have been bitter about the twists of fate and knee that ended his 1996 season prematurely. Going into the season, he was the Packers' third star, the Lord of the Leap, sharing the preseason cover of *Sports Illustrated* with Brett Favre and Reggie White. He was coming off a sensational season, 102 receptions for thirteen touchdowns and a team-record 1,497 yards, a fitting successor to his fellow South Carolina Gamecock, All-Pro Sterling Sharpe, a worthy heir to Don Hutson and James Lofton, the great Packer receivers of the past. Suddenly, seven games into the season, Brooks was finished. He was nobody.

He handled sudden obscurity as well as he had handled sudden fame. He kept a low profile, allowed his teammates to savor their own success. And yet he showed up to work every day, to work on the rehabilitation of his knee without crying or complaining. He strained, sweated, and smiled at his teammates. "I want them to see there's no quit in me," he said.

How frustrating was it for him to be on the sidelines?

"It's not frustrating at all," Brooks insisted. "Those guys are playing for me, also."

Coincidentally, Brooks, Freeman, and Beebe, the three prime wide receivers at the start of the season, were all drafted in the third round. So was Bart Starr's favorite target, Boyd Dowler, three decades earlier.

> After Sam Mills intercepted Favre's pass, Lamar Lathon, another Carolina linebacker, stuck his face in Brett's and said, "This is gonna be a long day."
>
> "We'll see," Favre said, mildly.
>
> When Lathon and the rest of the Panther defense trotted off the field, the Packer defense trotted on. Reggie White settled in at one end of the defensive line, Sean Jones at the other.

Sean Jones, who lugs his cellular phone almost everywhere except to the line of scrimmage, is a successful investment counselor, who, during the off-season, works and resides in Beverly Hills.

Lamar Lathon is one of Jones's clients.

Jamaican by birth, Jones is an uncommonly intelligent and diverse human being. He's owned a restaurant, started a clothing company, hosted a television show, served Thanksgiving dinners to the needy, created a foundation to motivate youngsters, and managed a hedge fund. His teammates say Sean is so smart he is almost as smart as he thinks he is. His teammates go to him for financial advice. They also go to him for food. His wife, Tina, serves soul food to the brothers every Friday night. His two-year-old son is the most visible child in the Packers' locker room. His son's

name is Dylan Sinclair Jones, which is nothing compared to Sean's full name: Dwight Andre Sean-O'Neil
Jones. He sounds like a whole investment firm all by
himself.

On the kickoff following Carolina's touchdown, Desmond
Howard darted through the Panther defenders, carried the ball
back 49 yards. He was brought down, finally, deep in Panther
territory.

Twenty-nine years earlier, Travis Williams, a Packer
rookie, performed similar magic on kickoff returns.
Williams *averaged* 41 yards for eighteen kickoff returns
in 1967. He returned four for touchdowns, one for 104
yards.

Howard's specialty is returning *punts*, not kickoffs.
In 1996, his first year in Green Bay, he returned fifty-
eight punts during the regular season for a total of 875
yards, an NFL record. One of his three touchdown returns covered 92 yards.

Desmond Howard came very close to being a Green
Bay Packer in 1992. He also came very close to *not* being a Green Bay Packer in 1996.

Mike Holmgren wanted to draft Howard in 1992.
Coming off a 4–12 season, the fifth worst record in the
NFL in 1991, the Packers had the fifth selection in the
draft. The Washington Redskins, coming off a Super
Bowl championship season, had the twenty-eighth
pick.

Joe Gibbs, the Redskins' coach, also wanted Desmond Howard. The Redskins traded up, acquired the fourth selection from the Cincinnati Bengals, and picked Howard.

The Packers then selected Terrell Buckley, a defensive back from Florida State.

Both the Redskins and the Packers ended up disappointed. Howard had one shining moment all season; he returned a punt 55 yards for a touchdown. Buckley had a few shining moments. He returned a punt 58 yards for a touchdown in an early-season game and an interception for a touchdown in a late-season game.

Howard and Buckley each lasted three seasons with the team that drafted him, neither coming close to fulfilling his promise. Both went south, figuratively and literally, Howard to Jacksonville, Buckley to the Miami Dolphins. Mike Holmgren and Ron Wolf both consider the drafting of Buckley in the first round their one major mistake in their first five years.

After the 1995 season, Howard became an unrestricted free agent. Holmgren remembered how close the Packers had come to signing him in 1992 and wondered if his judgment then was sound or faulty. Green Bay signed Howard in July 1996, partly because Holmgren was curious and partly because Howard came cheap. He signed for $300,000.

The Packers never made a wiser investment.

But in training camp, Howard was hampered by a hip pointer, missed the first exhibition game, and feared that he would not get a chance to showcase his skills. In the second exhibition, against the Pittsburgh

Steelers, he returned a punt 77 yards for a touchdown.
If there ever was a harbinger . . .

The week before the Carolina game, in the divisional
playoff game against San Francisco, Howard returned
two punts in the first six minutes for 71 and 46 yards,
the first for a touchdown, the second setting up a
touchdown and a 14–0 lead. Desmond's timing was
impeccable—for a half.

But when the 49ers kicked off to start the second
half, Desmond, who was supposed to be fielding the
kick, was still in the locker room. He was pulling on a
fresh uniform, replacing one that had been lashed by
the freezing rain in the first half. By the time Howard
realized he was expected on the field, it was too late.

The Packers misplayed the kickoff, San Francisco
pounced on the ball, and a swift touchdown threatened to turn a one-sided game into a contest. (Favre
promptly deflected that threat with a twelve-play, 72-
yard drive that devoured the clock and the 49ers'
chances.)

Howard's tardiness, of course, was a coach's nightmare, which Mike Holmgren didn't need. He already
had his own related and recurring nightmare. In his
dream, Holmgren kept trying to get to the field, to
reach the sidelines, but someone, or something, always
stopped him, held him back. Holmgren, like all
coaches, is at least part psychologist, and he says you
don't have to be as wise as Freud to interpret his dream.
"I'm sure it comes from frustration, from the fact that

my football career, my playing career, didn't turn out the way I wanted," Holmgren says. "I wanted to play college football, but I didn't get to play a lot. I got hurt my senior year. I wanted to play professional football, but I got cut. I couldn't get into the ball park."

Holmgren was drafted in the eighth round in 1970 by the Saint Louis Cardinals, who already had two capable quarterbacks in Jim Hart and Charley Johnson. When the Cardinals released him, the New York Jets gave Holmgren a shot. His first day with the Jets, he threw passes to Don Maynard and drank beers with Joe Namath, two future Hall of Famers. In between, a group of spectators asked him to sign autographs.

"Get up there, get his autograph," Holmgren overheard a woman telling her young son.

"Who is that, Mom?" the boy said.

"We don't care," the mother replied. "Get up there."

Holmgren's ego survived. He thought enough of his chances to rent an apartment in New York, but when the Jets were able to sign an experienced quarterback to help back up Namath, Holmgren had to break his lease.

His father then invited Mike to join him in the real estate business. His father and a pair of partners had established the first Century 21 office in Northern California.

"I really didn't want to go into real estate," Holmgren said, "but I went to school, took the test, all that stuff, got it done, for him, for my dad. I loved him."

Holmgren's father died very young. One of his partners, Dick Loughlin, went on to become president of Century 21 International, then invested in an NFL team. Loughlin owned a small share of the Carolina Panthers.

When his father died, Holmgren fled from the real estate business and instead became a high-school coach and teacher. In 1970, the year Vince Lombardi died, Mike Holmgren was coaching football and teaching history at Sacred Heart High School, a Catholic school in San Francisco.

Twenty-five years earlier, Vince Lombardi was coaching football and teaching chemistry at Saint Cecilia's High School, a Catholic school in New Jersey.

Holmgren's rise through the coaching ranks was, like Lombardi's, steady, not spectacular. He spent ten years coaching high school football, five years coaching college football, six years as an assistant with the San Francisco 49ers, three as the quarterbacks' coach under Bill Walsh, three as the offensive coordinator under George Seifert.

Lombardi's experience was eerily similar. He spent eight years coaching high school football, six coaching college football, and five as an assistant with the New York Giants, as the team's offensive coordinator in fact if not in title. Lombardi was forty-five when he became head coach of the Packers. Holmgren was forty-three when he took the same job. They even had the same astrological sign: Lombardi's birthday was June 11, Holmgren's June 15. Geminis. Twins.

*   *   *

The assistant coaches Holmgren assembled in Green Bay, many of them men he had gotten to know in stints at Brigham Young and in San Francisco, had their own links to Packer history. Sherman Lewis, the offensive coordinator, says he was "a big Packer fan" in the sixties for two good reasons: His hometown and his college. Lewis, like Paul Hornung, came from Louisville, and, like Herb Adderley, played both running back and defensive back for Michigan State. As Adderley's Spartan career ended, Lewis's began.

When he went to work for Bill Walsh and the 49ers in the early eighties, one of Lewis's fellow assistants was Norb Hecker, who had been an assistant to Lombardi in Green Bay. "I used to ask Norb what it was like during those days," Lewis recalls. "I wanted to know why Lombardi's former players never said anything bad about him. I wanted to know how he could be a hard, tough disciplinarian who yelled and screamed and still commanded respect.

"Hecker said he treated everybody fairly. No one got special treatment. He was a very religious man with very strong convictions. And he was a great motivator."

Lewis says that his Packer running backs, Edgar Bennett and Dorsey Levens, remind him of Paul Hornung and Jimmy Taylor. "They're not flashy speedy types, either," he says.

When Lombardi was molding the Packers into champions, Fritz Shurmur, Holmgren's defensive coordinator, was starting his coaching career at his alma mater, Albion College, an hour's drive west of Detroit. He witnessed a few of the classic Thanksgiving Day matchups between the Lions and the Packers. "Vince's teams were tough, physical teams," Shurmur says. "Our guys measure up. Our guys are tough and physical, too."

Do any of them remind Shurmur of Ray Nitschke?

"Wayne Simmons is very close to being as mean as Nitschke," he says. "He enjoys picking people up and throwing them to the ground."

When Bob Valesente played defensive halfback for Ithaca College in the early 1960s, he watched Herb Adderley play defensive halfback for the Green Bay Packers. "I was a Packer fan," Valesente says, "and I knew I wanted to be a coach. I wanted to grow up to be Vince Lombardi."

When Valesente arrived in Green Bay thirty years later, first to coach Mike Holmgren's linebackers, then the defensive backs, he promptly paid a visit to the stadium. "I wanted to walk on the same sideline that Lombardi walked on," he says.

Then Valesente crossed the street to visit the Green Bay Packer Hall of Fame. The smallest city in pro football is the only one that has its own Hall of Fame, which exists, and thrives, precisely because of the minuteness of the city and the magnitude of its football tradition. The Packer Hall of Fame, brimming with memorabilia, offers a stunningly rich visual and oral history of Packer football. You can see the four retired jerseys, of Canadeo, Hutson, Starr, and Nitschke; you can hear Vince Lombardi delivering speeches. The Hall of Fame is *the* major tourist attraction in Green Bay, luring 160,000 visitors in 1996. There is no Statue of Liberty to compete with, no Golden Gate Bridge, no Texas Book Depository.

"I wanted to see and hear everything that had anything to do with Lombardi," Valesente says.

Tom Lovat, the offensive line coach, knew a couple of Lombardi's Packers as opponents and teammates. As a freshman at the University of Utah, he played against Jerry Kramer, and as a senior, he played with Marv Fleming. Later, Lovat served as an assistant to Bart Starr in Green Bay.

Larry Brooks, the defensive line coach, played for the Los Angeles Rams against Bart Starr's Packers during the seventies, the lean years. "Back in the days when I played," Brooks says, "if management didn't like you, they said they were gonna send you to Green Bay or Buffalo. It was like a punishment. No one wanted to go to Green Bay. Mike and Ron changed all that. Now it's the place to go."

Mike and Ron—and Bob.

Bob Harlan, a journalism major at Marquette University, and sports information director at his alma mater during the Lombardi years, put in eighteen years in the front office of the Green Bay Packers before he was elected president and chief executive officer in 1989. He waited more than a year before he made the key moves that rattled and revived the franchise.

First Harlan hired Michael Reinfeldt to be the Packers' chief financial officer. Reinfeldt was hardly the typical bean counter. He had an M.B.A., but he also had an advanced degree in football. The only graduate of the University of Wisconsin–Milwaukee ever to play in the NFL, he was a defensive back tough and talented enough to last nine seasons and to be named Player of the Year in the American Football Conference in 1979. Two years after he stopped hitting people, Reinfeldt became chief financial officer for Al Davis's Los Angeles Raiders. He knew football, he knew money, and more important in the age of free agency and the salary cap, he knew how to juggle the two.

Next Harlan hired Ron Wolf, who was not the typical general manager. Wolf had not played football in college or in the NFL. But he had spent much of his adult life working for Al Davis, learning football and footwork, rising from researcher to personnel director of the Raiders, working with Mike Reinfeldt in Los Angeles. When Harlan picked Wolf to run the football side of the Packers, he told him, "You're going to have complete control over football operations. No interference."

Wolf thought, *That's kind of like being an owner,* and promptly started acting like one. He fired the coach, Lindy Infante, even though Infante's contract still had three years to run. Then Wolf set out to find a new coach. Several teams had expressed interest in Mike Holmgren, which was understandable. Bill Walsh's protégés had great track records. Wolf invited Holmgren to Green Bay, escorted him through the Packers' headquarters, showed him the banners, the names of the Hall of Famers, the portraits of Lombardi, the Lombardi Trophy. Holmgren not only seemed comfortable with the Packers' past; he seemed energized by it. He found the ghosts friendly. *This is the perfect guy*, Wolf thought. *I can work with this guy. I've got to get him.* Wolf offered Holmgren the job and promised, "I'll never go out and get you a player you don't want."

Holmgren had never been a head coach at the collegiate or professional level. He had once been rejected by the University of Montana, and he had rejected the New York Jets and the Phoenix Cardinals. But Green Bay appealed to him. He liked the idea of no owner. He liked the challenge of a team with a 4–12 record. Bill Walsh took over a 49er team that was 2–14 and won three Super Bowls. Vince Lombardi took over a Packer team that was 1–10–1 and won two Super Bowls. Holmgren decided that he, a Walsh guy from the 49ers, would be comfortable with Wolf, a Davis guy from the team across the bay. Harlan, the president of the Packers, not only didn't interfere; he didn't even meet Holmgren until Wolf had hired him.

Wolf and Holmgren had met before, in Hattiesburg, on the campus of Southern Mississippi, in 1991, at a workout spotlighting the skills of a senior quarterback named Brett Favre. Wolf represented the New York Jets at the time, Holmgren the 49ers. Favre's size, his strength, and his arm impressed both men. Holmgren recommended that the 49ers, who already had Joe Montana and Steve Young, draft Favre, but warned, "He throws every ball with the same velocity whether it's a five-yard pass or a forty-yard pass. He's really got to learn to discipline himself."

Holmgren's postworkout interview with Favre worried him, too. "What are you gonna do now?" Holmgren asked the young athlete.

"Drink some beer and chase some women," Favre said.

The trip to Hattiesburg in the heart of the Deep South was a bit of a culture shock for a man who had grown up in the cultured counterculture of San Francisco. "I felt like something out of *Easy Rider*," Holmgren recalls.

A year later, when Holmgren rode into Green Bay, Wolf said, "You remember Favre?"

The week Wolf joined the Packers, he had accompanied the team to Atlanta just so that he could watch the Falcons' rookie quarterback warm up. He had decided then he wanted Favre. Badly.

Holmgren remembered the kid's arm and his eyes lit up.

"You want him?" Wolf said.

"He can be a good one," the coach said.

On February 10, 1992, one month after hiring Holmgren, Wolf traded a first-round draft pick to the Atlanta Falcons for Brett Favre.

The delicate and treacherous process of building a winner had begun.

*   *   *

The process gained considerable momentum the following year.

After eight seasons with the Philadelphia Eagles, Reggie White, certainly the best defensive lineman in football, probably the best defensive player and arguably the best player, became an unrestricted free agent in 1993. He was free to go to any team in the NFL.

White announced that he was going to go wherever God wanted him to go. San Francisco and Washington both raised their hands.

Most people thought God would want Reggie to go to San Francisco. Even Reggie thought for a while that God wanted him to go to San Francisco.

San Francisco offered an inner city, a potential congregation for Minister White. San Francisco also offered $19 million, spread over five years, a potential bonanza for Minister White.

When the Green Bay Packers asked Reggie and his advisers to pay a visit to Wisconsin before he made up his mind, Reggie agreed only reluctantly.

Then Wolf, Holmgren, and his defensive coordinator, Ray Rhodes, went to work on White. "Reggie White is already a great football player," Wolf told White. "If you come here and play for the Green Bay Packers, you'll become a legend."

Reggie said he had to talk it over with God.

Holmgren called White's answering machine and left a message: "Reggie, this is God. I want you to play in Green Bay."

White was amused by Holmgren's message. "Thank

goodness," Holmgren says. White was moved by Wolf's.

The Packers offered White a four-year package worth $17 million. White figured out that that came to $4.25 million a year, higher than San Francisco's bid of $3.8 million a year. Moreover, Green Bay was willing to pay $9 million the first year, half in signing bonus, half in salary; San Francisco planned to backload its payments.

White also figured out that Holmgren and Rhodes had both come to Green Bay from San Francisco. Perhaps God meant He wanted Reggie to go to *San Franciscans*. Perhaps Reggie hadn't heard Him quite right.

Brett Favre joined in the pursuit of White. "I told him this was a great football town," Favre says. "I told him he could make the difference. I also told him I didn't want him hitting me anymore."

Reggie agonized over the decision, prayed over the decision, and when he made up his mind, Wolf's and Holmgren's prayers were answered. Reggie, in consultation with God, chose Green Bay.

Instantly, he gave the Packers credibility. Instantly, everyone in football knew that the Packers were serious about wanting to win, serious about being willing to spend money. Instantly, Green Bay turned from Siberia to Shangri-La, from everyone's Waterloo to everyone's Xanadu.

(Confession: I stole the last line. I stole the idea to contrast Waterloo—Napoleon's place of defeat—and Xanadu—Coleridge's place of idyllic beauty—from Walt Frazier, the former New York Knick star who now, as the team's radio broadcaster, loves to analyze in rhyme. Waterloo/Xanadu was Frazier's greatest moment.)

Reggie also gave the Packers an attitude. "I hate losing," he says. "Losing ties my stomach in a knot. It follows you around and destroys your sleep. It torments you. And I let guys know, 'If losing does not torment you, move on. Go play for somebody else.' "

After White, the deluge: Wolf and Holmgren drafted Wayne Simmons and Earl Dotson the same month, Aaron Taylor and Dorsey Levens the next year, Craig Newsome, Brian Williams, Antonio Freeman, William Henderson, and Adam Timmerman the following year. They traded for Keith Jackson in 1995 and for Eugene Robinson in 1996. They grabbed Santana Dotson and Desmond Howard as unrestricted free agents in 1996.

They built a contender, and they never could have done it so swiftly, and so solidly, if Reggie White had chosen to sign with San Francisco.

Reggie is a large and easy target for the skeptical. Does he really have chats with God? Does God know the difference between a defensive end and an outside linebacker? Does God care? God knows. But I know that in December 1995, Reggie White suffered a hamstring tear so severe the Packers announced his season was over; he would not be able to play in the NFC playoffs. The next day, a Thursday, Reggie announced that he would play on Saturday, that God had healed the tear. I spoke to the team doctor, and he said there was no way, medically, the hamstring could have healed, no scientific rationale for Reggie's recovery. Reggie wasn't surprised. He said it was the third time God had healed him.

A month before the Carolina game, as White's four-year commitment drew toward its close, the Packers offered him a new contract with familiar numbers: Five years for $19 million, precisely what San Francisco had bid in 1993. Reggie signed. At thirty-five, he is not likely to play till the end of the contract, but the offer did what it was designed to do: It made Reggie feel amply appreciated and compensated. He would receive a $3 million bonus plus a $2 million salary in 1997, his reward for being a player, a leader, a recruiter, and a symbol.

Reggie said he was also a cheesehead. He said the people of Wisconsin had shown so much love for him, his wife, his children, and his church that he was moving to the state, establishing residence not far from Milwaukee. Packer fans had donated more than $200,000 to help rebuild the church that had been torched in Tennessee. "These people believe in me," Reggie White says. "They believe in my integrity."

"So many young players today are so misguided, so misdirected, you need a Reggie White," Willie Davis says. "It's too bad every team couldn't have a Reggie White."

*   *   *

For twenty-five years, from the end of Lombardi's reign to the start of Holmgren's, the vast majority of football players did not want to live in Green Bay, did not want to play in Green Bay. The prevailing feeling was that the team was going nowhere and the town was already there. The only players even mildly attracted to Green Bay were hunters and fishermen, who knew that deer and trout were plentiful.

For black players, especially the single ones, the outdoor sports did not make up for the lack of black women in Green Bay, no Black Entertainment Television, no soul music on the radio stations, no redeeming social life, and from first game to last, no warming rays.

When James Lofton of Stanford University was drafted by Green Bay in the first round of the 1978 draft, he inquired about the racial environment. "They told me there were a thousand black people in Green Bay," Lofton says. "What they didn't tell me was that nine hundred of them were in the state penitentiary."

A decade later, when Deion Sanders came out of Florida State, some of his friends gathered in his room on draft day and chanted for the TV cameras, "No way, Green Bay, no way, Green Bay." (Dallas, choosing first, took Troy Aikman; Green Bay, choosing second, heeded the chant and tapped Tony Mandarich. The Sanders boys, Barry and Deion, went third and fourth, to Detroit and Atlanta. Ron Wolf, obviously, was not making the picks for the Packers in 1989.)

But now Green Bay has become a beacon for football players who want to win, no matter the color of their skin. Black players can carry the music they want with them. They can hang out in Xtremes and a dozen other clubs. They can date interracially without more than occasional stares and glares. A few of the current black players are married to white women, and they and their families are accepted, welcomed in Green Bay. They can rent or purchase homes anywhere in town.

This does not mean that Green Bay has become a racial paradise, a billboard for brotherhood. It does mean that the overwhelming majority of people in town love the Packers, and the only colors that deeply matter to them are green and gold. Otherwise, Green Bay is still, like most of Wisconsin, except for Madison and Milwaukee, the college town and the big city, a conservative area where people's perceptions of blacks have long been based on what they read and what they see on television and movie screens, not on experience. (There is no history of overt racism in Green Bay, no horror stories of blacks being abused physically or financially, probably mostly because there have been few, if any, blacks to abuse.)

Wolf and Holmgren have tried to make the town and team as comfortable as possible for their black players. Once a week, they bring in a barber from Milwaukee who knows how to cut African-American hair (drastically clipping the income of Robert Brooks, who used to shear his teammates' locks). Twice a week, they bring in caterers from Milwaukee to serve fried chicken, macaroni and cheese, collard greens, and black-eyed peas, the hardy and tasty fare that passes as soul food. Four of the assistant coaches, including the offensive coordinator, are black and at least one of the owners. Willie Davis owns one share of Packer stock.

The image of racial harmony among the Packers, which Holmgren and Wolf had worked so hard to nourish, was threatened late in the 1996 season when ESPN, in a generally flattering "Outside the Lines" portrait of Green Bay and the Packers, suggested that many of the team's black players were unhappy and uncomfortable in the community.

On ESPN, LeRoy Butler said he didn't like being called Reggie White or Sterling Sharpe. Robert Brooks said he objected to being asked which one are you? Sterling Sharpe, the retired receiver turned ESPN broadcaster, said in Green Bay, "I was a nigger." Sean Jones said being black in Green Bay is the same as being white in Harlem.

Butler's complaint and Brooks' were minor ones. Both of them balance their complaints with compliments for the city. "Everything here is football," Butler says. "No pro basketball. No pro baseball. Just the Green Bay Packers. We love it."

Sharpe never demonstrated any desire to be a part of the Green Bay community, any interest in developing fans or friends. He had about as much use for the people of Wisconsin as he had for the media. As a player, he refused to speak to reporters. Still, thousands of Green Bay fans showed their dislike of Sterling Sharpe in a strange way; they wore Packer jerseys with his number on them. And the media response was equally curious; after injury cut short Sharpe's career, ESPN hired him as a commentator.

Sean Jones's remark demands amplification. He would have been more accurate if he had said: Being black in Green Bay, *if you're a Packer*, is the same as being white in Harlem, *if you're Larry Bird*. In Green Bay, Packers are heroes, larger than life or color.

Still, it's logical that black Packers feel they are being scrutinized in Green Bay, feel they are, as Antonio Freeman says, "under a microscope," or, as LeRoy Butler says, "under a telescope." They *are* being stared at. Celebrities are always stared at, when they are recognized by their fans. Bill Cosby is stared at; so is Billy Crystal. Robert Brooks is stared at; so is Robert De Niro. It comes with the territory, with the fame and fortune. The difference, I suppose, is that when you're black, you're not always sure that's why they're staring.

Mike Holmgren was furious with the ESPN report. He urged his players, and his staff, not to cooperate with the cable network.

"I think this is the greatest town in America to play pro football," says Johnny Holland, who is an assistant coach and a former Packer player whose career, like Sterling Sharpe's, was ended by a neck injury. "Especially for a black player. There's nothing here outside of football, and that brings our players closer together."

In 1996, in contrast to the Dallas Cowboys particularly, and professional athletes generally, the Green

Bay Packers seemed like model citizens. Drug busts? Vice raids? Not in Green Bay. The Packers seemed more like Albert Schweitzer than Albert Belle.

Why?

"The bad things are just not here," LeRoy Butler said.

"There's not a lot to get in trouble with," Antonio Freeman said.

Still, as Desmond Howard pointed out, "You can always find mischief if you look hard enough."

There are bars galore in Green Bay. There are also strip joints, though not galore. The strippers in Green Bay are, frankly, not a vintage crop. They may be Milwaukee rejects.

It is not impossible to get messed up in Green Bay. It just isn't easy.

The players on most NFL teams try to get together one night a week. On some teams, the offense and defense socialize separately; on others, the whole squad gathers. In Green Bay, the players don't see each other one night a week. They see each other almost every night. They can't avoid each other.

"If I go to the grocery story for a quart of milk," Mark Chmura says, "I'm likely to run into a teammate."

How little is there to do in Green Bay? Sean Jones, who is computer-friendly, and Desmond Howard, who is learning, sent e-mail letters to each other almost every day during the 1996 season. "Honey, it must be real boring up here," Keith Jackson told his wife, "if these two guys see each other every day and then go home and e-mail each other."

Holmgren, who was the only white player on his high school basketball team, is, like Lombardi, very close to being color-blind. When he was trying out for the St. Louis Cardinals, one of his two roommates was black, the other a Texan. Once, when Holmgren asked to borrow the black roommate's comb, the Texan stared at him and shook his head. Holmgren stared back and combed his hair.

Dorsey Levens and Travis Jervey, black-and-white running backs, room together on the road, and so do Eugene Robinson and Mike Prior, black-and-white defensive backs. (Just as Jerry Kramer and Willie Davis did in the sixties.) Still, as on all professional sports teams half a century after Jackie Robinson, blacks tend to socialize with blacks, and whites tend to socialize with whites.

This is Green Bay, not utopia.

The Packers try to make life in Green Bay as attractive as possible for all their players, black and white. In training camp, the team offers a program called "Invest in Yourself," which encourages career and financial planning; attendance is mandatory for rookies. In addition, Sherry Schuldes, the Packers' director of family planning, works with the players' wives and children, counseling them on housing and schools, doctors and dentists, getting them involved in the community.

The Packers are not trying to be sociological trail-blazers. They are trying to win.

> The field position Desmond Howard had given the Packers with his kickoff return was wasted when Chris Jacke missed a 46-yard field goal attempt. The Packers kept struggling on offense, especially Favre. He completed only two of his first eight passes for a total of merely 15 yards. He looked tight. "He doesn't get tight," Mike Holmgren said afterward. "He does get too excited sometimes."

A month after Wolf acquired Favre, he signed Frank Winters, a little-known offensive lineman who had drifted among three different teams, the Browns, the Giants, and the Chiefs, during an undistinguished NFL career. He was primarily a long-snapper for punts and placements; he had started only six games in five years.

A month later, Wolf drafted Mark Chmura from Boston College. Like Favre and Winters, Chmura was not exactly labeled can't miss. He was not selected until the sixth round of the draft; 156 players were considered better prospects.

Winters and Favre met for the first time at a spring minicamp. They sat down to eat at the same table in the dining room. Neither had a clue who the other was.

"What position do you play?" Winters asked Favre.

"Quarterback," Favre said.

Winters wondered if Favre was putting him on. Brett weighed more than 240 pounds at the time. Winters thought he was a linebacker.

Chmura suffered a back injury a couple of months later, spent the entire season on injured reserve, and considered quitting so seriously he once packed his bags and got as far as the parking lot before Holmgren persuaded him to stay.

Can you imagine the odds against those three guys from Mississippi, Massachusetts, and New Jersey becoming best friends, becoming known as Green Bay's version of "The Three Amigos?"

Probably almost as high as the odds against Favre, Chmura, and Winters all, eventually, making the Pro Bowl.

One spring Chmura and Winters went to visit Favre at his parents' home at the end of a dirt road in Mississippi, and their host invited them to join him on a little pontoon boat in a nearby swamp. "He asks us if we want to go swimming," Chmura says, "and me and Frank are like, 'No way!' So Brett jumps in and we go about a hundred yards upstream and we see a beaver with no head on it that's just been eaten by an alligator. And he's out there swimming with water moccasins, and me and Frank are just sitting in the boat, holding on, saying, 'There's no way in hell we're goin' into that water.' It was disgusting."

Shit be bringin' it, hoss!

Winters brought some awareness of Green Bay's past with him when he became a Packer. "Sure, I knew about Lombardi," he says. "There was a Lombardi rest stop on the New Jersey Turnpike."

Antonio Freeman knew Packer history, too. "I had heard of Brett Favre and Sterling Sharpe," he says. He had also heard that it was cold in Green Bay.

> The Packers stifled Carolina's running game in the first quarter, limited the Panthers' longest run to 3 yards. Up front, in between Jones and White, Gilbert Brown provided run-stopping girth and left the pass-rushing to Santana Dotson.

In the early sixties, in the heart of the Lombardi dynasty, Willie Davis used to return to his alma mater, Grambling University, to assist his old coach, Eddie Robinson, during spring practice. Davis, who was only the second man from Grambling to play in the NFL, soon discovered another prospect at the Louisiana school. "He was a big guy, a strong son-of-a-gun," Davis recalls. "I thought he was going to be the next great lineman out of Grambling."

The lineman's name was Alphonse Dotson, and in 1965, the year the Packers won the first of three straight titles, Vince Lombardi, perhaps prodded by Willie Davis, chose Alphonse Dotson in the second round of the NFL draft. But Dotson elected to sign with the Kansas City Chiefs of the rival American Football League. He was traded to Miami *before* the Chiefs played the Packers in Super Bowl I. He was then traded to Oakland *after* the Raiders played the Packers in Super Bowl II.

The year of Super Bowl III, Alphonse Dotson became a father and named his son after a wise Indian chief.

"Santana—the Winston Churchill of Indian chiefs,"
Alphonse Dotson says.

Santana Dotson went to Baylor, then was drafted by
Tampa Bay. In 1996, after four losing seasons with the
Bucs, Dotson elected, as an unrestricted free agent, to
sign with the Green Bay Packers, the team his father
had once rejected.

"Big shoes to fill," Santana Dotson said, after he met
some of his father's contemporaries during Alumni
Weekend in Green Bay. "We're just trying to put our
feet in and fill 'em up with tissue paper."

Amazingly, three of the Packers' four defensive linemen had the same birthday. White, Dotson, and Jones
were all born on December 19, although not in the
same year. Gilbert Brown shared his birthday, February
22, with George Washington, also not in the same
year.

Transylvanians approached Count Dracula's castle
no more warily than visiting teams approach Lambeau
Field. In five years under Holmgren, going into the Carolina game, the Packers had won thirty games at Lambeau and lost only four. They had won twenty-seven
of the last twenty-eight, including the last seventeen
in a row. Going back to Lombardi's days, the Packers
had played eight postseason games in Green Bay and
had won all eight. "We know where the soft spots are,
the slick spots," Frank Winters explained.

Topography wasn't the answer. Nor were the ghosts,
or the climate, although both helped. The real secret
was the crowd, the most durable, loyal, forgiving fans

in the world. They scorned the controlled comfort of a dome. They embraced their team even in defeat. They considered the Packers their neighbors, their friends, their family. They had bought every available ticket for every game for twenty-seven years, 176 straight games. The ticket prices were fan-friendly, the lowest in the NFL in 1996, at an average of $30.61 apiece.

The stadium cost less than a million dollars to build in 1957, a $960,000 bargain, the cost shared by the Green Bay Packer Corporation and the City of Green Bay, which now owns the park and leases it to the club (at a rent of $1.2 million annually, the city clears $500,000 a year). The stadium held 32,150 fans at its opening, but in the next decade, three separate expansions swelled capacity to 50,852, not one view obstructed, every seat aluminum and backless. In more recent years, the addition of private boxes and theater-style club seats—*indoor* seats with *backs*, a sure sign of the decay of midwestern civilization—increased capacity to 60,790.

For the Carolina game, the Packers sold 60,790 tickets.

The week before, the Packers sold 60,790 tickets for the San Francisco game and announced that 60,787 were used, that only three timid ticketholders were frightened away by the freezing rain. Packer fans are macho, but not quite *that* macho. A media scramble to identify the three no-show wimps quickly produced half a dozen unused tickets, and Fuzzy Thurston said he had a couple more that a friend had not picked up.

The odds are that at least twenty people chickened out, maybe thirty.

The count was probably more accurate for the Carolina game. The Packers admitted that 574 tickets were not used.

On December 31, 1967, Lambeau Field offered seating for 50,852 fans. But, officially, 50,861 people, nine beyond capacity, attended the Ice Bowl (and another million said they did). The people of Green Bay must've been tougher in the sixties.

Pamela Geurtz missed the Ice Bowl, but she had a good excuse. She was seven months old. When she was born, in May 1967, four months after Super Bowl I, her father submitted an application in her name for season tickets. Twenty-seven years later, just in time for the 1994 season, her tickets came through. She went straight from the Lombardi era to the Holmgren era, bypassing the frustrating seventies and eighties.

Now, more than 25,000 people are on a growing waiting list for season tickets, and only a handful become available each year. Unless attrition accelerates dramatically, or Lambeau expands geometrically, the wait for Packer tickets now is far more than a thousand years. Pamela Geurtz was born at the right time.

In 1996, Pamela moved from Green Bay to Seattle, Washington. She flew home, of course, to use her season tickets to see the Carolina game.

Tom Wetts attended the Ice Bowl. He was thirteen

years old, and he and his two brothers climbed a fence and squeezed into end-zone seats next to their parents. Twenty-nine years later, Wetts, who was living in Cincinnati, flew to Green Bay for the Carolina game. On the plane and at the stadium, he thought about his grandfather Harold. Harold Wetts had been dead for a decade, but Tom thought about him every time he went to a Packer game. Harold had willed his season ticket to his grandson. Tom said he loved his grandfather Harold very much and would never forget him.

Tom's two brothers went to the Carolina game, too. Their mother and father, still season-ticket holders, had given their tickets to their sons as Christmas presents. The boys couldn't imagine better presents. They couldn't imagine better parents. Nothing brings families together in Green Bay quite like the Packers.

Pamela Geurtz and Tom Wetts are clearly *avid* Packer fans, but not *unusual* ones. Judy Smith has had season tickets in her family for sixty years. She has lived in San Diego for almost twenty years but still flies back to Green Bay for games, three of them in 1996. Gordon Doxtater has had season tickets for fifty-five years and has missed only one game, a meaningless season-ending contest against Pittsburgh in 1967. But the Packers lost that day, and Doxtater hasn't taken a chance on missing a game since. For forty-seven of the fifty-five years, Doxtater lived in Chicago and commuted to Green Bay for the games.

Green Bay fans do have limits. John Lambeau's

grandmother, who was one of Curly Lambeau's three wives, still lives in Green Bay and still cheers for the Packers. But John says that, at ninety-seven, grandma has stopped going to the stadium that carries her name.

Going to games is only one part of being a Packer fan. "How do you explain going to bed thinking about the Packers?" a fan named Dennis Noack once asked me. "How do you explain dreaming about the Packers? How do you explain waking up thinking about the Packers? There's nothing like it."

How do you explain a lifetime draped in green and gold? At Bellin Memorial Hospital, at Saint Mary's and at Saint Vincent—which is, to some people's surprise, *not* named after Lombardi—newborns are sent home in caps knitted in Packer colors.

Joel and Jennifer Demerth were sent home with matching Packer jackets when they were married. Jennifer, who paints her fingernails green and gold, says the jackets were their favorite wedding present.

The Wisconsin Vault & Casket Company, headquartered in Janesville, advertises "THE LIMITED EDITION—GREEN AND GOLD CASKET"—in the *Packer Report*. Right next to the coffin coupon is an ad for "THE GREEN BAY EXPERIENCE," an annual football fantasy camp. Many baseball teams offer fantasy camps, a chance to hit and pitch against major leaguers. Some basketball teams offer fantasy camps, a chance to jam and jump against NBA heroes. But only Green Bay offers a football fantasy camp. *A chance to be tackled by Willie Davis and blocked by Jerry Kramer?* Sounds like a terrific way to drum up business for Wisconsin Vault & Casket.

In fact, The Green Bay Experience, five days for $3,495, which covers hotel, meals, mementos, liniment, and bandages, is a safe and, for Packer fans, unbelievably satisfying experience. Neither Davis nor Kramer nor Starr nor Wood nor Thurston hits anyone. Mostly, they tell stories, many of them truthful, about the Lombardi era. They spread nostalgia, and Mike Holmgren and Brett Favre stop by and say hello, the past and present blending as they do so regularly in Green Bay. The highlight of the camp is the re-creation of the play that decided the Ice Bowl.

The green-and-yellow-brick road that winds from cradle to matrimony to grave in Wisconsin is lined with temptation. You can buy Packer parkas, Packer T-shirts, Packer undershorts, Packer sweatpants, Packer hats, Packer ties, Packer ponchos, Packer blankets, Packer headbands, Packer helmets, Packer helmet lamps, Packer car flags, Packer coffee mugs, Packer wallets, Packer key chains, Packer golf balls, Packer club covers, Packer tire covers, Packer checkbook covers, Packer watches, Packer cribbage boards, Packer teddy bears, Packer ice buckets, even Packer players for public appearances (weddings, birthdays, *bar mitzvahs*), everything except—sorry, Scarecrow; sorry, Tin Man—a Packer heart or a Packer brain. Seventy million dollars worth of Packer paraphernalia was sold in the first month of 1997, lifting Green Bay from a midseason merchandising ranking of fifth in the NFL to second, behind only the Dallas Cowboys, the kings of capitalism.

Want something a little different? How about a Tundra Terrarium, if you're into dirt? A cheesehead? Swiss or American? Or, slightly more exotic, a brathead? A Packer helmet signed by Brett for $325? An NFL football signed by Brett for $175? A Number 4 jersey signed by Brett and framed for $499? Prefer Reggie? Same items, different jersey number, same prices. How about a lithograph? Seven faces of Lombardi in vivid color? The Lombardi Sweep, with Kramer and Thurston escorting Taylor? Lambeau Leap? Take your choice: Robert Brooks or The Butler Did It.

Don't forget your pet: Green-and-gold leashes, collars, sweaters, and caps available for an astonishing number of dogs named Reggie or Brett. A local farmer names his cows after quarterbacks; Brett and Bart were both barnyard busts, modest milk producers. Another farmer paints his barns green and gold; his version of an Amish hex sign is a Packer helmet.

If the Packers are worth writing home about, you can do it on Packer postcards—1966 team picture? Lambeau landscape?—or Packer stationery slipped into Packer envelopes. And now you can even lick a Packer stamp, Lombardi's visage, part of the series that includes the former Alabama coach Bear Bryant and the former Chicago Bears coach George Halas. "The Lombardi stamp has the Halas stamp beat all to hell," one

Packer partisan typically insisted when the postal service unveiled the stamps. "They shouldn't even have a
Halas stamp."

Packermania proliferates on all fronts. Music? During the 1996 season, you could hear such nifty numbers as "Cheezeheads Rule" or "The Pack Is Back," or
catch CWA—Cheeseheads with Attitude—singing
"Cheesehead Baby" or the Tennessee Ernie Ford spin-
off, "Sixteen Games." Plus, of course, the "Packarena."
Who could forget the lyrics? "Brett, Brooks, Edgar and
a Reggie/Jackson and Chmura and Holmgren and a
Jacke/Jones and a LeRoy and a Newsome and a Dorsey/
Hey, Packarena!" Who could remember the lyrics? To
accompany the words, you do The Forward Pass, The
Catch, and The Spike.

Nothing to do in Green Bay? Ridiculous. Larry Primo
of De Pere plotted the perfect social schedule in 1996.
Monday nights, he drove his green-and-gold van to the
Coaches Corner, to sit in on a Packer radio show. Tues-
days, he hit the Stadium View for another Packer program. Wednesdays, he moved quickly, to catch one
show at The 50-Yard Line, another at Knights on Main
(where Brett Favre used to tend bar occasionally and
charm customers, as he delivered their drinks, by head-
butting them). Thursdays, presumably, he rested, or
patronized more of Green Bay's countless sports bars:
The Glory Years, The Goal Post, The Stadium Lounge,
The Townline Sports Pub, Gipper's Sports Bar, GB
Sports Bar, Time-Out Sports Bar, all decorated, sort of,
in Packer Classic, Packer Modern, or Packer Mixed.

Mike Holmgren's weekly TV show lured overflow crowds to its Monday morning tapings at WBAY-TV and even larger audiences on the air. *The Mike Holmgren Show* ranked among the ten most watched TV shows in Wisconsin, between *Suddenly Susan* and *Spin City*, well ahead of *NYPD Blue*. Brett Favre's show, naturally, was a blockbuster, too, but you didn't have to be a quarterback, or even a star, or even playing, to have your own show. Aaron Taylor, an offensive guard, the most anonymous of positions—"the perfect place to hide out from the law," Jerry Kramer once suggested— had a radio show *and* a TV show. Defensive tackle Bob Kuberski, a Naval Academy graduate who dressed for two games all season and played in only one, settled for his own radio show. George Koonce, Eugene Robinson, injured Robert Brooks, everyone had a microphone in his mouth. Packer fans embraced all Packers, big names or small, stars or scrubs. Terry Mickens, far down on Favre's list of busiest receivers, drew a capacity crowd to a Quarterback Club luncheon and earned an ovation for endorsing heartland values. "I hold a dollar till it hollers," Mickens said.

Rick Harnowski is a Polish-born artist who operates a tattoo parlor on Broadway. Broadway, *Green Bay*. Rick can do exquisite, intricate work, a Vietnam scene, for instance, entitled "Living Hell on Earth," which spreads across an ample gut and captures vividly the horrors of war. But his customers lean toward Packer logos and Lombardi Trophies. One of Rick's recent assignments is a portrait of Mike Holmgren, with the face of Lombardi looming, almost ghostlike, in the background.

If Harnowski is the town's master tattoo artist, Chad Loch is the master canvas. His commitment to the Packers is indelible: His skin sports a Packer helmet, a view of Lambeau Field, a Lombardi Trophy, a Lombardi portrait, and a picture of Brett Favre in action, not quite life-sized. Loch is the walking Prado of Packerland, the Louvre of Lombardi Avenue.

Isolated instances of insanity? Hardly. The Green Bay Packers were mentioned on the front page of the Green Bay *Press-Gazette* every day for five weeks before the Carolina game and every day for three weeks afterward. December 7, 1996, through February 2, 1997. You could look it up. It's difficult to imagine, say, the Giants on the front page of *The New York Times* for even three days in a row. Or the Bears on the front page of the *Chicago Tribune* for more than a couple of days.

With five minutes to play in the first half of the Ice Bowl, Green Bay's 14–0 lead seemed a comfortable one. But in the next three minutes, Bart Starr and Willie Wood, both future Hall of Famers, fumbled deep in their own territory. The Cowboys recovered both fumbles, converted them into a touchdown and a field goal, and cut the margin at halftime to four points, 14–10.

For most of the twentieth century, the rivalry between the Chicago Bears and the Green Bay Packers was among the fiercest and most famous in American sports. They were two of the NFL's original teams (although the Bears were called the Chicago Staleys in 1921, the league's first official season). Their founders were formidable men, both players and coaches, Curly Lambeau and George Halas, who dueled with each other, on the field and off, for more than thirty years. They were geographically close—some 200 miles from Lambeau to the Loop—and they played each other at least twice a year every season from 1925 on. They won more NFL championships than any other teams; the Bears owned nine, only two fewer than the Packers, going into the 1996 season. Their fans hated each other. Their players weren't too fond of each other, either.

But the Bears and Packers have not met in a postseason game for more than half a century, and the Dallas Cowboys have replaced, or at least challenged, the Bears as the team that Green Bay fans love to hate. This does not make Green Bay fans unique. The Dallas Cowboys, like the old New York Yankees, inspire hatred from coast to coast.

The Cowboys and Packers played for the first time in 1960, the year the Cowboys were born. The Packers crushed the Cowboys the first three times they played, then faced them in the 1966 NFL championship game, for the right to represent the league in Super Bowl I.

The game was a beauty. Bart Starr passed for four touchdowns, and in the final minute Tom Brown, the Deion Sanders of his day, a big-league baseball player turned defensive back, intercepted a Don Meredith pass in the end zone to preserve a 34–27 Packer victory. The rivalry really began then and grew heated in the Ice Bowl.

In the seventies and eighties, the teams collided infrequently, only once in Green Bay, only once in a playoff game, and the rivalry cooled. The Cowboys won nine divisional titles in the two decades, the outmanned Packers only one.

Then in the 1990s, when Wolf, Holmgren, and Favre revitalized Green Bay, the one team the Packers could not beat, the only team they could not measure up to, was the Cowboys. In 1993, 1994, and 1995, the teams met twice a year, all six times in Dallas, three regular-season games and three postseason games, and the Cowboys won all six games.

The Cowboys got the regular-season games at home because of the vagaries of NFL scheduling; they got the playoff games at home because they earned it, because they had a better record than the Packers each year.

Every defeat was painful for Green Bay and its fans, but none so painful as the NFC championship game on January 14, 1996, the Packers' first title game in twenty-eight years. The Packers had won eight of their previous nine games. They had won the last four in a row, and their victims included the defending Super Bowl champions, the San Francisco 49ers, and the team that would go on to represent the AFC in the Super Bowl, the Pittsburgh Steelers. Brett Favre, coming off an MVP season and an almost flawless performance against the 49ers, had not thrown an interception in four games, one hundred and twenty-five passes without one being picked off.

Favre threw three touchdown passes against the Cowboys, two to Robert Brooks and one to Keith Jackson, and the Packers took a 27–24 lead into the final quarter. They could taste the Super Bowl. But then Favre and the Packers ran dry, and Emmitt Smith ran wild. Smith scored two touchdowns in the fourth quarter, the second set up by the second of two interceptions Favre threw, and Dallas won, 38–27.

The Cowboys went to the Super Bowl.

The Packers went home.

During the flight back to Green Bay, Reggie and Brett and their teammates made a promise to each other. They promised they would be flying to New Orleans a year later.

On the final play of the first quarter, the Packers suddenly sprang to life. Dorsey Levens burst through a huge hole on the right side—Jeff Thomason, the Packers' *third* tight end, simply wiped out Kevin Greene, one of the Panthers' All-Pro linebackers—then cut to the sideline and raced for 35 yards before Eric Davis shoved him out of bounds on the Carolina 29-yard line.

On the first play of the second quarter, Favre lofted the ball toward the right side of the end zone, and Levens, racing out of a slot to the right, again found himself in a duel with Davis. Both men went up, and this time Levens won, snaring the ball, keeping both feet in bounds, a nifty catch, evening the game at 7–7.

The Packers and the Cowboys met midway through the 1996 season, paired in the glaring spotlight of ABC's Monday Night Football. Once again, the NFL's scheduling formula sent the Packers to Dallas.

Only ten days earlier, the game had seemed almost a mismatch. The Packers were 8–1 then, the Cowboys 5–4, no better than third in their division, trailing Washington and Philadelphia, who were both 7–2. Another defeat, and the Cowboys probably could forget about retaining their Super Bowl championship. One more defeat, and they might even have to forget about getting into the playoffs.

But the Cowboys, who thrived on pressure, used the wall that pressed against their backs as a catapult. The week before the Monday night confrontation, the Cowboys beat the 49ers in San Francisco in overtime. The same day, the Packers, perhaps looking ahead to Dallas, showed up flat in Kansas City and absorbed their second defeat of the season. Cornerback Doug Evans, one of the mildest of the Packers, was thrown out of the game for protesting an interference call too strenuously. Worse, Mark Chmura went out of the game with a foot injury, a partially torn arch.

The Packers' best blocking tight end joined the team's best receivers, Brooks and Freeman, on the sidelines. Favre took the blame. "I put myself at risk the way I play," the scrambling quarterback said, perhaps half kidding, "and I sometimes put my receivers at risk, too. I'm killing these guys."

Don Beebe, the gritty veteran from Chadron State, winding down his pro career at the age of thirty-one, and Derrick Mayes, the glittery rookie from Notre Dame, starting his at the age of twenty-two, caught passes from Favre for the Packers' two touchdowns in Kansas City.

For the Packers, the Dallas game was enormous, a mini–Super Bowl, or more, a test of their fortitude and their potential. The *Press-Gazette* called it a "make or break" game, and the players did not argue. "It's hard to go into the beast's kingdom and get a victory," Santana Dotson said, "but it's something we must do."

If the Packers were the best team in football, if they were the team that was going to win the Super Bowl— and they believed they were—then, the experts said, they had to beat the Cowboys. They had to defeat the team that, for three years in a row, had wiped them out short of the Super Bowl, the team that had won an unprecedented three Super Bowls in four years. If they lost, their credentials were tarnished, their credibility suspect. In reality, it was the Cowboys' season, not the Packers', that would be devastated by a defeat, but the popular perception among fans and media was that the Packers had more at stake, more to prove.

Mark Chmura raged against the injury that would keep him from participating. "It stinks," he said. "I just mope around the house. It's gonna be tough to even watch the game."

He also raged against the Cowboys. "I hate Dallas," he said. "I can't stand 'em." Chmura said he hated their coach, detested their writers, despised their players. He didn't even have a kind word for their cheerleaders. "Michael Irvin and I went to the Pro Bowl last year," Chmura said, "and we were teammates, and his locker was right next to mine, and I didn't say one word to him the whole time. It's the cockiness about them, the flash. Everybody on this team hates 'em."

"You must love Deion," I said.

"Oh, yeah," Chmura said. "He's a real good friend of mine."

Chmura glowered. "And they're not better than us, I don't care what anybody says. They're no better than we are."

Ironically, several of Chmura's teammates—including Edgar Bennett, LeRoy Butler, Brian Williams, Antonio Freeman, and Bob Kuberski—-had grown up as Cowboy fans. They got over it.

Brett Favre respected the Cowboys, respected them on the football field. "They've played great against us," he said. "They're good."

Could the Packers beat the Cowboys?

"I figure if we play them often enough, eventually it's got to go our way," Favre said, then smiled. "I may be saying that in ten years, too," he added.

Favre certainly did not sound overconfident, and when his comments were repeated to his coach, they may have been slightly distorted. Holmgren heard that Favre was asked, "Will you ever beat them?" And Holmgren heard that Favre replied, "I don't know."

"What are you, out of your mind?" Holmgren asked his quarterback. "Do you really believe that?"

Brett reassured Holmgren, assured him that he did think the Packers could beat the Cowboys. Holmgren's interpretation was that Brett was just feigning uncertainty, that he was kidding, making a small joke. "My read," Holmgren said, "is that Brett thinks he's Jay Leno, so he'll throw out things for a little chuckle now and then."

Holmgren didn't chuckle. He *hoped* Brett was just kidding.

How big was the game?

"It's pretty important," Favre said. "I'd hate to go back there in January again."

A Dallas sportswriter named Skip Bayless, who is equally talented and opinionated, stirred up a small storm by disparaging Reggie White's aging skills. "Against Erik Williams," Bayless wrote, "he might as well be *Betty* White." Reggie was stung by the comparison; Betty White may have been, too, but she kept her own counsel. Bayless's Cowboy newsletter, *The Insider*, pointed out that in the Packers' six straight defeats in Dallas, White had made only eleven tackles and had no sacks. Bayless rubbed it in, called the Packer leader "Reggie Black-and-Blue." When White indicated that he wouldn't mind going one-on-one with Bayless, the slender journalist said that might be the only matchup Reggie would win.

"Reggie White is the best football player I've ever seen," Brett Favre countered. "In the back of our minds, we want to win this for Reggie."

Troy Aikman, the Dallas quarterback, shared Favre's opinion that he and his teammates played exceptionally well against Green Bay. In the two games against the Packers in 1995, Aikman had completed 70 percent of his passes, forty-five of sixty-four, for 571 yards and four touchdowns. "I just seem to have my best games against Green Bay," Aikman admitted.

Aikman claimed he did not know how many times in a row Dallas had beaten Green Bay. The answer was seven, going back to a game in Milwaukee in 1991.

Holmgren and Favre, however, were only 0–6.

The morning of the Dallas game, Martha's Coffee Club gathered at the Bay Family Restaurant near Lambeau Field, a coterie of longtime Green Bay fans who, through the glory days and the gory days, met each weekday morning to talk Packer football. They fretted about Dallas. "Chmura's injury, that hurts a lot," one old-timer suggested.

"Every team has injuries," someone else said. "You gotta overcome it."

"We gotta get some turnovers. We haven't had any turnovers lately."

"Dallas'll take it to us at the end of the game. They always do."

"Why do we have to play 'em down there every year?" someone complained. "They haven't been here since 'sixty-seven."

Actually, Dallas had come to Green Bay once since the Ice Bowl. In 1989, the Packers beat the Cowboys at Lambeau.

"I think we're all as confident as can be," said one faithful fan.

"It's not the end of the world if we lose," said another.

To a certain extent, the game between the Packers and the Cowboys shaped up as a morality play, good against evil, a Western in cleats instead of boots, the blue-collar work ethic of Green Bay against the oversized glitz of Big D, Reggie White and the saints marching in against Michael Irvin and the sinners. That, of course, was oversimplification. There were players on both sides who did not fit the formula. Still, oversimplification is a staple of American journalism, especially what passes for journalism on television, and the Cowboys and Packers were expected to play their assigned roles.

The battle was not only to determine who would be the favorite to win the Super Bowl. The battle was to determine who would be the *favorite, America's* favorite, America's team. The Cowboys had long usurped and enjoyed that designation, but in the wake of drug busts and sex scandals, real and alleged, of rampaging ego and hypocrisy and arrogance, there was rumbling, and not only in the Midwest, that the Green Bay Packers, not the Dallas Cowboys, were really America's team.

Which raises two pertinent, if impertinent, questions:

1. Is being called "America's Team" really a compliment in this sporting age of greed and entitlement?

2. How can any team committed to greed and entitlement not be called "America's Team"?

To nettle the Packers, Jerry Jones, the Dallas owner, and Barry Switzer, his hired gun, urged Cowboy fans to cheer lustily and wear white, but the patches of white around Texas Stadium simply made the clusters of green and gold stand out. No team attracts so many supporters to road games as the Packers do. Some Packer fans choose to travel because they can buy tickets more readily in cities like Seattle and Detroit and Tampa, for instance, than they can in Green Bay. Others choose to travel for a respite from the Wisconsin winters or the Green Bay grind. Most choose to travel simply because they love the Packers. Many planned vacations around the game against the hated Cowboys. The majority came from Wisconsin, but a few journeyed from each coast, and more from Texas. They sure loved their bratwurst barbecues. *Shit be bringin' it, hoss.*

Of the 65,000 fans in Texas Stadium, a conservative guess was that at least 10,000 were Packer fans. The team's old guard was represented by Max McGee, who was broadcasting; by Donny Anderson, who was entertaining customers; and by the old guard, Fuzzy Thurston, who was escorting a traveling pack of Packer backers.

None of the Green Bay fans found much to cheer about.

The game started and ended with Barry Switzer making a statement. At the beginning, for the coin toss, he sent out safety George Teague and linebacker Fred Strickland, who had been Packers the previous year, to serve as two of the Cowboy tri-captains against their former teammates. Then, in the final thirty seconds of play, with Dallas comfortably in command, 18–6, Switzer called a timeout so that he could dispatch Chris Boniol to kick his seventh field goal in seven attempts and equal a National Football League record.

Reggie White, frustrated all night, limited to three tackles and no sacks, exploded when Switzer called the timeout, bolted across the field toward the Cowboys' bench, pointing his finger and screaming the sort of words and sentiments that he would never dream of expressing from the pulpit. Even some of Switzer's own players argued against going for the field goal—they saw it as adding insult—but after the game, after Boniol's record field goal made the final score 21–6, a subdued Reverend White said that he might have overreacted.

Some of the Packers remained belligerent. "I want to get 'em in Lambeau," Santana Dotson said. "I want to play them again," Mike Holmgren said.

Reggie White and Brett Favre were not so eager.

"They won, they beat us," White said. "That's what it boils down to."

Favre, battered and limping, was even more succinct. "The bottom line is they kicked our butt," he said.

"The Packers had all but said this was their Super Bowl," reporter Richard Justice wrote in the *Dallas Morning News*. "At least it was a chance to prove that they belonged in one. They didn't even get close."

"Maybe in another Ice Bowl, or another Ice Age, Green Bay will beat the Cowboys," columnist Randy Galloway gloated.

"The Packers still aren't in the Cowboy-49er league," Skip Bayless opined.

Neither Green Bay nor Dallas scored in the third quarter of the Ice Bowl, but on the first play of the fourth quarter, the Cowboys struck. Dan Reeves, who would later coach Denver in three Super Bowls, took a pitch from Don Meredith and threw an option pass to Lance Rentzel, a bold play that covered 50 yards and gave Dallas a touchdown and the lead, 17–14.

Suddenly, eleven games into the 1996 season, the Packers were no longer the clear favorites in the National Football Conference. With five games to go, San Francisco and Washington matched Green Bay's 8–3 record, and Dallas, Carolina, and Philadelphia were all within one game of the leaders. The prevailing wisdom among the so-called experts was that Dallas had the momentum, the experience, and the pure talent—Irvin, Aikman, Smith, and Sanders—to win the Super Bowl. And if the Cowboys stumbled—rumors of impending arrests pursued the team like groupies—then perhaps the Denver Broncos, at 10–1 the team with the best record in football, were ready to end the AFC drought, to break the NFC's string of twelve straight Super Bowl victories. It was a frightening, almost heretical thought.

The only consolation for the Packers was that the defeat in Dallas led directly to the acquisition of Andre Rison. Which proved to be a considerable consolation.

Carolina soon regained the lead, a Favre fumble setting up a Panther field goal. Favre promptly retaliated. He led the Packers on a 71-yard scoring drive that lasted fifteen plays and ate up almost eight minutes. Edgar Bennett carried the ball five times for 28 yards, and Favre polished off the drive by completing his seventh pass in a row, floating the ball into the arms of Antonio Freeman for the touchdown and the lead, 14-10.

The touchdown pass was the sixteenth Favre had thrown in postseason play, breaking the Packer record of fifteen set twenty-nine years earlier by Bart Starr in Super Bowl II.

Edgar Bennett and LeRoy Butler have known each other since they were teenagers in Jacksonville, Florida. They played together at Robert E. Lee High School, at Florida State University, and in Green Bay. Butler, who is seven months older, joined the Packers in 1990, drafted in the second round. Two years later, he urged the Packers to draft Bennett, who was picked in the fourth round.

Butler and Bennett, best of friends, are proof that opposites attract. Butler grew up in the projects in Jacksonville, Bennett in the suburbs. Butler plays defense, Bennett offense. Butler demands attention; Bennett shies away from it. Butler's Mercedes is white, Bennett's a more conservative black. When Butler wants new clothes, a tailor flies in from Beverly Hills. When Bennett wants new clothes, he favors sweats and a baseball cap. Butler oozes confidence, Bennett insecurity. When Dorsey Levens began gaining yards and playing time midway through the season, Bennett first suspected the media was lining up against him, then suspected coach Holmgren was trying to phase him out. He stopped talking to reporters; he continued talking to his coach.

Bennett and Butler share a work ethic that has enabled both of them to beat the odds. When Butler was a child, he suffered from a bone disorder that, for a time, confined him to a wheelchair and forced him to wear braces on his legs. When he discarded the chair and the braces, he drove himself to run faster than anyone else. At Florida State, he was an All-American defensive back, a year behind Deion Sanders and two years ahead of Terrell Buckley, who were also All-Americans. Deion trained LeRoy; LeRoy trained Terrell.

When Butler was drafted by Green Bay, he thanked Lindy Infante, who was then the coach, and asked him only one question: "Where exactly is Green Bay?" Once he found the town, he often called Bennett in Tallahassee and told him how cold it was. "Guess what, LeRoy?" Bennett would needle. "It's eighty-five down here." Then Bennett would laugh. He stopped laughing when the Packers drafted him.

Bennett, his college career detoured for a year by injury, came out of Florida State with Buckley. Terrell was the star, the blue chip, the center of attention in the

Packers' training camp. Bennett, more accomplished as a blocker than a runner, was overlooked, almost ignored. He played sparingly in his rookie year, but by his fourth season, he became the fifth 1,000-yard rusher in Packer history. The first two were Hall of Famers Tony Canadeo and Jimmy Taylor.

Neither Butler nor Bennett smokes or drinks. But they are not entirely without vices. Two weeks before the Carolina game, they both bet big on their alma mater, Florida State, against Florida in the Sugar Bowl. They both gambled and lost.

In the final minute of the first half, Carolina's Kerry Collins gambled and lost. His long pass was picked off, an acrobatic one-handed interception by a Green Bay rookie named Tyrone Williams. Favre then completed two quick passes for 48 yards, and Chris Jacke kicked a field goal to put Green Bay in front at the half, 17–10.

Tyrone Williams came very close to spending the day of the Carolina game in prison.

In 1994, when he was an undergraduate at the University of Nebraska, Williams fired two shots into an occupied car. None of the passengers was injured, but in 1996, after Williams pleaded no contest, he was sentenced to community service, alcohol-free probation, and six months in jail. He was supposed to start serving his sentence December 3, but Williams appealed, and his prison tour was pushed back to February, after the Super Bowl. With good behavior, Williams would be released in time for training camp. He wouldn't miss a single practice. Remarkably, when Nebraska won the 1994 and 1995 national collegiate championships, Williams, despite his legal problems, never missed any of their games, either.

The star of those Nebraska teams, the quarterback Tommie Frazier, came to the Carolina game to cheer for Williams. Like Bennett and Butler, Williams and Frazier had gone through high school and college together.

Williams was one of four rookies who suited up and played against Carolina. One, John Michels, the first-round choice, had started at offensive tackle for most of the regular season. Another, defensive end Keith McKenzie, was a seventh-round draft choice from Ball State, which is better known for its David Letterman than for its football lettermen. The fourth rookie, safety Chris Hayes, was lucky on two counts: First, that he had been cut by the New York Jets, the worst team in football, two weeks before the regular season began, and, second, that he had been activated by the Packers, the best team in football, two weeks before the regular season ended.

Midway through the NFC championship game, the streets of Green Bay were practically empty, stripped of motorists and pedestrians. But not everyone was glued to the football game. Seven people preferred the matinee at the Bay 3 movie theater. Four were watching *Mighty Ducks 3*, and three *The Associate. Dear God* played to nothing but empty seats. John Juchemich, an usher in the theater, said he didn't mind missing the game, he wasn't much of a football fan.

The president of the Green Bay chapter of the Chicago Bears Fan Club, Scott McDaniel, watched the game on television and rooted for the Panthers. McDaniel was born in Chicago, but raised in Wisconsin. "A lot of people around here can't stand the Packers," he insisted. "You'd be surprised."

Scott claimed to have thirty members in his club. His wife, Christy, was not one of them. She was a Green Bay native and a Packer fan, and when Scott was identified on local television as a Bears fan, she was embarrassed. "I didn't want anyone to know he belonged to me," Christy said.

"I don't think she's ever going to join," Scott lamented.

Don Beebe and Lindsay Knapp of the Packers, both born in Illinois, both grew up rooting for the Bears. They probably weren't going to join, either.

Knapp's parents, ironically, were born in Wisconsin and grew up Packer fans, so dedicated they both attended the Ice Bowl. His mother suffered frostbite at the game.

Fourteen months later, Lindsay was born. There was probably no connection.

"The harder you work," Vince Lombardi told his players, *"the harder it is to surrender."* He also said, *"Fatigue makes*

cowards of us all." In the fourth quarter of the Ice Bowl, Lombardi's Packers fought off fatigue and flatly refused to surrender.

Herb Adderley, the Hall of Fame cornerback who once said, "I think of Vince Lombardi every day of my life, and I loved my father, who is also deceased, but I don't think of my father every day," watched the Carolina game at the home of his girlfriend, Pam Gray. Pam wore a Dallas Cowboys jacket, a Christmas present from Herb, through the whole game. Pam was a Cowboys fan. When the Cowboys played the Packers during the regular season, Herb and Pam bet a dinner on the game, but did not watch it together. Herb was too avid a Packer fan. "I was a Packer fan," he says, "even when I was playing for the Cowboys."

At the start of the second half against Carolina, Green Bay drove 73 yards in eleven plays, mixing runs and passes almost evenly, keeping the Panther defense off balance. The key plays came on third down, a pair of passes that kept the drive alive, one to Don Beebe for 29 yards, one to Dorsey Levens for 8.

The play to Levens was spectacular, Favre at his innovative best. On third and seven, Kevin Greene, the Carolina linebacker, bolted at Favre and wrapped his arms around him, and as Brett was going down, he pushed the ball with two hands, a chest pass to Levens. Dorsey, hit as he charged upfield, fumbled, then recovered his own fumble, with a yard to spare for the first down.

Once again, a Carolina linebacker had something to say to Favre. ``Wow!'' said Kevin Greene.

When the drive sputtered inside the Panthers' 20-yard line, Chris Jacke kicked a field goal to extend the Packers' lead to 20-10.

On the radio, Max McGee called Bret Favre "the man."

"He's the kind of guy you'd like to play with, isn't he?" said McGee's broadcasting partner, Jim Irwin.

"Absolutely," McGee said. "I'd even like to go out with him at night."

The Mayor of Green Bay, Paul Jadin, was able to get a ticket to the Carolina game. He was not able to get a ticket to the Ice Bowl. "I was very poor growing up," Paul Jadin says. "I didn't see a Packer game in person until I was about twenty."

He *heard* the Ice Bowl—most of it. "Everyone knows where they were for the Ice Bowl," Jadin says, "and ninety per cent of the people will tell you they were there. I was at home listening on the radio, and my radio went out, so I called a friend to find out what was going on, and he said we were losing with sixteen seconds to play and hung up. I thought it was over and started crying and praying.

"I prayed that they would come back, that there would be a miracle, and I promised God that if the

Packers won, I would become a priest. When I found out that they *had* won, I started bargaining with God so that I wouldn't have to become a priest. Maybe just a politician."

Jadin, a good politician, likes to say that the Packers are to Green Bay what the Eiffel Tower is to Paris. "They're our landmark," he says. "They're our identity. Could we survive without them? Certainly. But would life be as good in Green Bay without the Packers? Certainly not."

The mayor of Green Bay deals regularly with the mayors of far larger cities, cities that have big-league franchises, cities that dream of having big-league franchises, cities that fear losing big-league franchises. He is treated with respect. "People assume that I come from a city of three hundred to five hundred thousand people," Jadin says. "The Packers allow us to play bigger than we are."

The Packers play big in the Green Bay economy, bringing in $50 to $75 million dollars a year. Hotel rooms. Restaurant meals. Cheeseheads. Beer. But the Packers are hardly the only flourishing business in the city. Green Bay is home to five Fortune 500 companies—Fort Howard Paper, Schneider National Trucking, American Foods, Packerland Packing, and Schreiber Foods.

Packerland is a meatpacking company that took its name from the football team, which took its name from a meatpacking company. (The Indian Packing Corporation put up the money for the team's first uniforms in 1919. Lambeau worked for Indian Packing while he ran, kicked, passed, and coached the fledgling Packers to ten straight victories by a combined score of 565–6. They lost their eleventh game, the final game of their first season, by a score of 6–0. The Beloit Fairies beat them.)

American Foods specializes in beef, pork, and seafood; Schreiber in cheese; and Fort Howard in tissue. Fort Howard is the main reason Green Bay is known not only as "Titletown," but also as "the toilet paper capital of the world." It is also one of the main reasons the Green Bay economy is remarkably resistant to business slumps. "Even in a recession, people need toilet paper," the mayor points out, "and food."

The impact of the Packers on Green Bay goes deeper than dollars, cuts right to the psyche of the city. The mood of Green Bay reflects the record of the team. People walk with a jauntier step when the Packers win; psychotherapists reported that their business slumped as the Packers surged in 1996. "If I'd been mayor in the eighties, life might have been difficult," Jadin says. "But now I love waking up as mayor of Green Bay, especially the day after we've beaten the crap out of the Bears."

The Packers affect the quality of life in the city in myriad ways. Slow students learn to read faster when they learn by reading the Monday sports section of the *Press-Gazette* ; they are motivated by wanting to know how the Packers won. Because the Packers are a world-class team, and a world-class organization, the rest of the town tries to measure up, to improve its products and services, diversions, and image. A new auditorium, the Weidner Center for the Performing Arts, houses concerts and theater, ballet and ice shows, featuring well-known actors and musicians and singers and skaters, maybe not quite in Brett's league, or Reggie's, but close.

Green Bay brings to mind the University of Oklahoma, when the school was known for its football and nothing more. "We want to build a university," the school's president, Dr. Harold Cross, once said, "that the football team can be proud of."

There is some of that in Green Bay.

Only one mayor of Green Bay ever went on to higher office. Dominic Olejniczak rose from mayor of the city to president. Not of the United States. Better. President of the Green Bay Packers. Olejniczak hired Vince Lombardi and presided over the glory years.

One of the great strengths of the Packers is that they do not have an owner. They do not have a George Steinbrenner to denigrate the players and coaches. They do not have an Art Modell or a Georgia Frontierre or a Robert Irsay to abandon the fans.

The Packers do have stockholders, 1,915 people who own 4,634 shares of stock. No one is allowed to own more than 200 shares, most own only one, and no one can sell even a single share for a profit.

The stockholders meet once a year, usually late in May, and elect the Board of Directors, which has forty-five members, one of whom is a woman. The Board, which meets four times a year, elects a seven-member

Executive Committee, which meets once a month. The Executive Committee elects the president of the Green Bay Packers. No one is paid, except the president and chief executive officer, Bob Harlan.

The stock was issued in 1950 at a face value of $25 a share. If a stockholder wishes to sell a share, he must sell it back to the corporation. For $25. The corporation will then resell it for $25. No more. No less. No profit. No loss. Bob Harlan owns one share. Ron Wolf would love to own a share, but doesn't. Mayor Jadin says he is looking for a share.

Stockholders can, and do, pass their shares along to their children, but the transaction must go through the corporation.

When the Packers began in 1919, they were not a nonprofit organization. But they were close. They played their games at an open field and passed a hat and, at the end of the season, divided the profits among the players. Each player collected sixteen dollars.

The Packers did not fare much better financially the following year, and even the birth of the National Football League in 1921 did not perceptibly improve the team's fortunes. The NFL's original twenty-one teams included the Rock Island Independents, the Rochester Jeffersons, the Columbus Panhandles, the Evansville Crimson Giants, the Tonawanda Kardex, the Muncie Flyers, and the Louisville Brecks; the only team that has participated in every NFL season under the same name in the same city is the Green Bay Packers. Yet the Packers almost didn't make it through 1922. The *Press-Gazette* had to advance them money to finish the season.

Their fans were already zealots; they then bled royal blue and gold, the team's original colors. In 1923, five hundred fans filled Turner Hall in downtown Green Bay to follow a recreation of the game the Packers and Bears were playing in Wrigley Field. Jim Coffeen, who had played on the 1919 team, received the play-by-play by telegraph and relayed it to the eager audience; onstage, a life-sized football moved up and down a downsized replica of a football field. History fails to record whether the spectators sang the team's fight song:

> *Go, you Packers, go and get 'em.*
> *Go, you fighting fools, upset 'em.*
> *Smash their line with all your might*
> *A touchdown, Packers, fight, fight, fight!*
> *Fight on, you Blue and Gold, you glory,*
> *Win this game, the same old story.*
> *Fight, you Packers, fight,*
> *And bring the bacon home to old Green Bay.*

Boffo ending in a meatpacking town.

In 1923, the Packers were incorporated for the first time, on a nonprofit basis, essentially to avoid taxes. During the Depression, the Green Bay Football Corporation went into receivership, and was replaced, in 1935, by the Green Bay Packers, Inc., whose bylaws stated: "The corporation shall be non-profit-sharing and its purpose shall be exclusively for charitable purposes . . . no stockholder shall receive any dividend, pecuniary profit or emolument by virtue of his being a stockholder . . . should there be a dissolution of the Green Bay Packers, Inc., the undivided profits and assets of the Green Bay Packers, Inc., shall go to the Sullivan-Wallen Post of the American Legion for the purpose of creating a proper soldiers' memorial."

The Packers struggled for solvency in the thirties and forties, then crashed in 1949. The team did not have enough money to finish the season. To raise funds, the Packers charged admission to an intrasquad exhibition game on Thanksgiving Day and persuaded their greatest player, the retired pass-catching wizard, Don Hutson, to suit up for the scrimmage. Despite a heavy snowfall, despite a mediocre team that was tumbling toward a 2–10 season, the people of Green Bay responded magnificently to the Packers' emergency. They gave. The Packers took in $50,000 in gate receipts for an exhibition, enough cash to complete the season.

The Green Bay Packers, Inc., decided then it was once again time to sell stock in the corporation. Curly Lambeau advocated a restructuring. He argued for turning the Packers from a nonprofit into a for-profit corporation. His viewpoint was understandable: Lambeau was one of pro football's pioneers, one of its driving forces, right up with Halas in Chicago and Tim Mara in New York and Art Rooney in Pittsburgh. He had devoted his life to the Packers. He looked like an owner, he felt like an owner, but he wasn't an owner.

But Lambeau's popularity in Green Bay had de-clined. Some people objected to his lifestyle and claimed he had gone Hollywood. Others objected to his coaching and blamed him for the decline of the team. The committee rejected Lambeau's proposal—he quit and defected to the Chicago Cardinals—and de-cided that the character of the organization should re-main the same, that the Packers should continue to be community-owned and nonprofit. The language of the new stock certificates struck a familiar note: "The holder hereof understands and agrees: That no divi-dend shall ever be paid in said stock, nor is the stock assessable; that if the corporation is dissolved, all the assets shall go to Sullivan-Wallen Post No. 11 of the American Legion for the purpose of creating a soldiers' memorial."

The Packers sold almost 5,000 shares and, armed with more than $100,000 in working capital, headed into the historic 1950 season, the season the NFL ex-panded by merging with the All-American Football Conference and absorbing three of its healthier teams, the Cleveland Browns, the Baltimore Colts, and the San Francisco 49ers.

Emil Fischer, the president of the Packers, was named president of the National Conference of the en-larged league. "All those rumors that Green Bay was going to be dropped out of the league ought to be laid to rest now," Fischer said. "It shows that the small town still is an important cog in this new machine."

In 1961, in the early days of the Lombardi era, when football was starting to challenge baseball in popularity, Commissioner Pete Rozelle persuaded the owners of the National Football League teams that it was in their best interest to sell the television rights to their games as a package, with all teams sharing equally in the revenue.

In 1994, the National Football League instituted a salary cap, limiting the amount of money each team could spend on its players.

If Curly Lambeau had not failed to persuade the Packers to become a commercial venture in the fifties, if Rozelle had not championed revenue-sharing in the sixties or if the NFL had not conceived the salary cap in the nineties, the odds are strong that the Green Bay Packers would no longer exist. Shared revenue—from TV rights and NFL merchandise—accounts for more than 80 percent of the Packers' total revenue.

A greedy owner, or, to be kind, a smart businessman, would have moved them to a more lucrative market, or the Packers would have been driven out of business because their income was too small (without the TV money) or their expenses were too great (without the salary cap).

The Sullivan-Wallen Post No. 11 would have its memorial by now, and Los Angeles or Cleveland or Podunk would have the Packers.

Instead, the Packers are still in Green Bay, and the franchise is estimated to be worth $165 million.

The odds are strong, too, that neither the NFL nor any major professional sports league will ever create or tolerate another Green Bay, a civically owned, nonprofit team. The present rules of the NFL permit a team to be owned by no more than twenty-five persons, one of whom must own at least 30 percent. The Packers predate the rule and are exempt from it.

"I think there is an aversion to dealing with government," Mayor Jadin says. "For some reason, they prefer to deal with a greedy owner."

Mayor Jadin watched the Carolina game not from his usual seat—he owns four season tickets, which he managed to get upgraded when he became mayor—but from the warm sanctuary of a private box. Not that Jadin couldn't have coped with the weather. But he was playing host to the mayor of Charlotte, Pat Mc-Crory, who was not accustomed to being exposed to 3 degrees above zero.

Green Bay got the ball back with 4:50 to play in the Ice Bowl. I was getting ready to leave the protective cover of the press box, to head down to the locker room. Jerry Kramer had told me Coach Lombardi had convinced the Packers that they never lost a game, but that sometimes the clock ran out when the other team had more points. Dallas was leading, 17–14. I decided that the title of the book Kramer and I were working on would be The Year the Clock Ran Out.

In the 1970s and 1980s, the relationship between the former Packers, Lombardi's Packers, and the active Packers, Dan Devine's and Starr's and Gregg's and Infante's, was not a good one. At the beginning, the older

Packers, some subconsciously, some consciously, didn't want to see the younger Packers duplicate or even approach their achievements. "It didn't bother me when they didn't win," Jerry Kramer admits. "I didn't want to see them erase our records and our memories and the whole Lombardi era."

Inevitably, as the teams of the seventies and eighties failed to come anywhere close to the success of the sixties, as the fans and the media increasingly spoke and wrote wistfully of the glory days, the younger Packers began to resent their predecessors. "I remember playing golf with Lynn Dickey," Boyd Dowler says, "and he'd say, 'Why don't you guys go away?' "

Larry McCarren, twice a Pro Bowl center, played twelve seasons in Green Bay, from 1973 through 1984, but only once, in the strike-shortened and -distorted season of 1982, did McCarren's Packers reach the playoffs. He got sick of hearing about the old team. " 'Back in the sixties, it was like this; back in the sixties, it was like that,' " McCarren says. " 'Lombardi would have done it like this, or that.' It gets to the point where you want to pull your hair out if you hear those phrases again. When you don't measure up, and we didn't, it really is tough."

James Lofton was the Packers' best player in the eighties, an All-Pro wide receiver for six straight years who broke Don Hutson's Green Bay records for passes caught and pass-catching yardage. Lofton knew the history of the Packers as well as any player of his generation, and valued it. He actually attended the first Super Bowl game as a child in Los Angeles. "I was immensely proud to play for that franchise," Lofton says. "I didn't resent the fact that the old Packers had been the best team ever. But I was humbled by it."

Lofton, playing under Bart Starr, once told his coach that, as a youngster in the schoolyard, he used to pretend he was Johnny Unitas, who was Starr's rival and Lofton's idol. One day, early in Lofton's career with the Packers, he was loosening up before a game against Baltimore when he heard Starr, standing behind him, say, "Can you believe this guy thought you were better than I was?"

Lofton turned around and saw Johnny Unitas standing next to Starr. "All of a sudden," Lofton says, "I'm not an All-Pro receiver anymore. I'm an eight-year-old kid again. I got up, I shook Unitas's hand, I couldn't say a thing. And I can still feel that tingling sensation to this day. I got to meet my idol, and it was facilitated by Bart."

Lofton wished desperately he could help Starr win a championship, help Green Bay win a championship. But, like McCarren, Lofton never played on a Packer team that won more than eight games in a season. His teams, too, came up short. *Back in the sixties . . . back in the sixties . . .*

As losing season followed losing season, as "Titletown" turned into a cruel joke, a bit of the luster may have come off the old Packers, their credibility tarnished, too; guilt by association. A generation grew up in Green Bay barely believing that the team had once been great, half-suspecting it was just another of the local Indian legends. The old Packers would return to

Wisconsin for golf tournaments and fund-raising dinners and find themselves apologizing for their succes-
sors. They began rooting with a little more passion, a
little more sincerity.

Then, with the arrival of Wolf and Holmgren and
Favre, the Packers began to win, to take steps first toward respectability, then toward dominance. "I"m getting excited, my heart's pumping, and I'm yelling and
yahooing," Jerry Kramer said.

Now the two generations have come together, the
players of the sixties, many of them in their sixties, and
the players of the nineties, many of them in their twenties. The old Packers have mellowed, their competitive
juices calmed; they catch glimpses of themselves in the
gifted young players and they cheer for them. The
young Packers are too young to compete with the distant past; only ten of the 1996 Packers were born before
Super Bowl I, and only two of them, Jim McMahon,
who was seven, and Reggie White, who was five, could
have even vague memories of the game. Starr and Davis and Hornung and Wood are not rivals; they are legends.

"They're good guys, the old guys," Mark Chmura
says. "They all know what's going on with the Packers.
They all know who's playing. They all want us to win."

Midway through the 1996 season, Chmura met Paul
Hornung for the first time. "We talked like we'd known
each other for years," Chmura says. "Here's a guy I'd
grown up hearing about. I'm starstruck in front of him,
and he's talking like we're equals. It's weird, 'cause we
don't think of ourselves as stars."

"The young guys, they realize we're really pulling for them," Willie Davis says. "I wasn't comfortable in the locker room in the past. I'm comfortable now. Holmgren and Wolf want us to be part of this."

"They're our biggest fans," Antonio Freeman says.

If the old Packers have a favorite among the young Packers, it is probably Brett Favre, with Reggie White a close second, and everyone else third, which makes the veterans, in their preferences, no different from the fans. "Brett Favre is a sweetheart," Jerry Kramer says. "He's polite, respectful, thoughtful. He treats us with a certain deference. There is no arrogance, no ego."

Fuzzy Thurston offers the ultimate compliment. "Brett could've been one of us," he says.

"Which one of the current Packers reminds me of me?" Ray Nitschke says. "Brett Favre." Nitschke thinks of Favre as a linebacker in a quarterback's body.

"If you and Hornung were several years younger, and Brett was a couple of years younger," I once asked Max McGee, "would the three of you be running together?"

"Absolutely," McGee said. "I just might use him as bait the way I once used Hornung."

When McGee was reminded that Favre already had running mates in Winters and Chmura, Max said, "They ought to invite me along. I'll pick up the tab."

McGee is a distinct rarity, one of the few NFL players from the sixties who could afford to pick up a tab for players from the nineties.

But, seriously, folks: "Brett Favre has handled a lot

of heavy pressure this year," McGee said, "and come out of it with no wounds that I can see."

Favre, like McGee, has a sense of humor, which certainly helped him get through the rigors of rehab after his addiction to Vicodin. Late in the season, after the St. Louis game, sitting in the training room, his ankle wrapped in ice, Brett turned to Dr. Patrick McKenzie, the team physician, and said, "Doc, Doc, I need some Vike. Just a couple. Please." Favre avoided taking himself too seriously while he avoided taking painkillers and alcohol.

Two nights before the Carolina game, during dinner at Favre's home in Green Bay, his seven-year-old daughter, Brittany, lifted her water glass and said, "A toast: Good luck to my daddy on Sunday!"

Her daddy couldn't resist the opening. "Hey," he said, "no more bourbon and Coke for you!"

Carolina challenged the Packers once again, forging a 73-yard drive capped by three straight Kerry Collins completions, carrying the Panthers inside the 10-yard line. But the Packer defense stiffened, and Carolina settled for a field goal. The Panthers trailed by only a touchdown, 20–13, late in the third quarter. They still had a chance.

Carolina kicked off, tackled Desmond Howard at the 26-yard line, then stopped Edgar Bennett after a 4-yard run. On second and six at the Green Bay 30, Holmgren, anticipating a blitz, called ``Seventy-four fullback slow screen right.'' The Panthers blitzed. Favre dropped back and looped the ball over the head of a charging Kevin Greene and into the hands of Levens, who cut through the Carolina defenders and, helped by a crisp block by Frank Winters, ran 66 yards, all the way to the Panthers' 4-yard line. ``The perfect call,'' said Carlton Bailey, one of the linebackers Levens beat. The play broke the Panthers' spirit, broke the game open.

If there was a single play that transformed the Packers' 1996 season, that set them on the road to the championship, it came in their twelfth game, against the Rams, in Saint Louis. Green Bay was coming off the defeat in Dallas, their second defeat in a row. Their bid for the home-field advantage in the playoffs was in jeopardy. Their 8–3 record was no better than the Redskins' or the 49ers'.

Saint Louis was 3–8, a dismal team with a dismal record. Still, at halftime, the Rams led, 9–3. The Packers had gone three games in a row without scoring a touchdown in the first half, without once taking a lead. Freeman, Chmura, and Brooks were still ailing. Rison was still learning the offense.

On the second play of the second half, cornerback Doug Evans, who had been kicked out of the Kansas City game, perfectly read a quick slant pattern, cut in front of the receiver, intercepted Tony Banks's pass, and ran 32 yards, untouched, to the end zone. The Packers took the lead, 10–9. They went on to win, 24–9, then ran the table, won their last four games in increasingly convincing fashion, and finished the regular season with a 13–3 record, earning the right, the *privilege*, to play at home throughout the NFC playoffs.

"When they look back on the season," Eugene Robinson said after the Saint Louis game, "they'll point to Doug's interception and say that's what turned it around."

Doug Evans grew up in a dirt-poor black family in a small town in Louisiana, which probably explains why his favorite television show is *Seinfeld*. He didn't see many people like Jerry or George or Kramer in his childhood. He probably thinks *Seinfeld* is a foreign film. Frank Winters, who grew up in Jersey, only a few miles from Manhattan, is available to translate.

During their surge at the end of the regular season, there were two developments that made the Packers a significantly stronger team. The first was the emergence of Dorsey Levens as a running threat. In the final four games, Levens gained almost as many yards as he had gained in the first twelve games, scored more touchdowns than he had scored in the first twelve games and averaged almost twice as many yards per carry. Levens, who had been basically a blocking back in 1995, and Edgar Bennett powered the Packers to more than 200 rushing yards in the final game against Minnesota, the first time the team had reached that level in more than two years.

The second development was the resurrection of the receiving corps. Freeman and Chmura both recuperated ahead of schedule. Freeman missed four games, Chmura only three, and both joined Rison in the starting lineup for the last three games of the season. All the pieces fell neatly in place for the playoffs.

William Henderson was set at fullback, the blocking back position, freeing Levens to concentrate on running, backing up Bennett at halfback. When Henderson joined the Packers, part of a glittering 1995 draft class that included four men who were starters in 1996, his ambition was to earn and save $30,000 so that he could go to graduate school and become a physical therapist. His swift success, so far beyond his expectations, had been tempered by tragedy. His mother died of diabetes during his senior year in college, and his fiancée was murdered after his rookie season in the NFL.

Dorsey Levens rested after his long run, and Edgar Bennett, following textbook blocking, burst through the right side of his line and dashed untouched into the end zone. The 4-yard run gave the Packers their fourth drive of the game of more than 70 yards. More important, they led, 27–13.

The Carolina Panthers, ranked eighth in the NFL against the rush, never dreamed that the Packers would run so powerfully against them, never dreamed that the Packers' blocking would be so effective. Green Bay's offensive line had peaked for the playoffs, blended at just the right time. "They're blocking better than ever," Brett Favre said.

Frank Winters, the center, the acknowledged leader of the offensive line, also led the Packers in nicknames. He started the season as "Porky," for the usual reason, then evolved into "Corky," when one of his teammates had trouble with his hearing. Winters also answered to "Johnny Roast Beef," which was my favorite, because the actor Johnny Roast Beef—maybe you remember him as Jimmy Caan's sidekick in *Honeymoon in Las Vegas*, or as the hoodlum Robert De Niro ordered killed in *Goodfellas* because he bought his girlfriend a Cadillac—is a friend of mine. The real Johnny Roast Beef, incidentally, is a football fan, and flattered to share his name with Winters.

Aaron Taylor and Adam Timmerman, the left guard and the right, came to the Packers in consecutive years, with identical initials and antipodal credentials.

Taylor was an All-American from Notre Dame, the winner of the Lombardi Trophy, presented to the best college lineman in the country. He was chosen in the first round of the 1994 draft, the thirteenth player selected.

Timmerman was from South Dakota State University, the winner of the Jim Langer Award, presented to the best Division II college lineman in the country. He was chosen in the last round of the 1995 draft, the 230th player selected.

The difference between Taylor's résumé and Timmerman's was, roughly, the difference between Lombardi's fame and Langer's.

(Langer is not exactly a nobody: He was the center

on the undefeated Miami Dolphins team of 1972 and he is the only player in the Pro Football Hall of Fame who attended South Dakota State University.)

But the highly-touted Taylor blew out his right knee in minicamp and sat out his entire rookie season. He came back and started every game the following year, but when he tore up his other knee in the first game of the playoffs, Timmerman, a rookie, moved into the starting lineup.

In 1996, both Taylor, finally healthy after two major knee operations, and Timmerman started every game, flanking Frank Winters. They competed against each other only for listeners. Timmerman hosted the popular Friday morning radio program, *Breakfast with the Boys*, while Taylor hosted the popular Monday night radio program, *The Aaron Taylor Show*. Timmerman's show told you what was going to happen on Sunday; Taylor's told you whether it did.

Since Timmerman wears Number 63, which was once Fuzzy Thurston's uniform number, and plays right guard, which was once Jerry Kramer's position, both of the old guards are big Timmerman fans. Which is only fair, because Timmerman's father was a big Thurston and Kramer fan. "My dad got hooked in the sixties," Timmerman says. "He lived in Iowa, and the Packers were *the* team."

When Fuzzy celebrated his sixty-third birthday the week before the Carolina game, Adam Timmerman and his wife attended the birthday party at Shenanigans, and the two 63s embraced. Adam toasted Fuzzy with his usual Coke. Fuzzy responded with his usual vodka.

The first time Jerry Kramer and Aaron Taylor met was at a Packer fantasy football camp. Taylor came to speak to the campers and counselors, and Kramer was impressed. "He was bright, articulate, and gigantic," Kramer recalls.

After Taylor's speech, he asked if anyone had any questions.

Willie Davis raised his hand. "Aaron," he said, "with your obvious physical gifts, and your mental abilities, it's possible that you could've been a defensive player."

Taylor looked at the old captain of the defense and said, "I had higher aspirations than that, Mr. Davis."

Kramer loved him immediately.

Still, during the Carolina game, Kramer concentrated on Timmerman, studying the man who was filling his shoes. "I pulled with him," Kramer said. "I moved with him. I blocked with him."

Earl Dotson, the right tackle, is the least conspicuous, least publicized member of the offensive line. Just as Jerry Kramer spent much of the sixties answering to "Ron," because of the higher visibility of tight end Ron Kramer, Earl Dotson is likely to be called "Santana." Earl, from Texas A&I, is so quiet that hardly anyone outside the team recognizes that he is the Packers' best offensive lineman. As Jimmy Breslin once wrote, about his favorite author, himself, "If you do not blow your own horn, there is no music."

*   *   *

The only unstable position on the offensive line was left tackle, the one position, ironically, that had belonged to one man for a decade. From 1986 through 1995, Ken Ruettgers started 139 games at left tackle; in five of those years, he started every game. He, LeRoy Butler, and the placekicker Chris Jacke were the only pre-Holmgren regulars who were still with the Packers.

But all his years in the trenches took a terrible toll on Ruettgers's left knee, and when training camp began in 1996, he couldn't walk without pain, couldn't practice, couldn't even make up his mind whether he wanted to play anymore. Gary Brown, who had played sparingly in his first two seasons, and John Michels, a rookie who had been a starter only during his senior year in college, competed for Ruettgers's job; when Michels sprained an ankle during the exhibition season, Brown won.

Brown played well in the opening three games, but none of the offensive linemen distinguished themselves in the fourth game, against Minnesota. Favre was sacked seven times, the most in his career, and Brown was sacked, too, dropped from the starting lineup. Michels, who was healthy, replaced him, a rookie assigned to protect the left side, the vulnerable side, of the league's Most Valuable Player.

Michels is, in many ways, a Ruettgers clone. They play the same position. They went to the same school, Southern California. They walk alike, they talk alike, they even think alike. They're both big fans of Rush Limbaugh. (Imagine a *defensive* lineman named *Rush*

• In an industrial city of barely 100,000 people,
everyone puts their faith in the Packers.

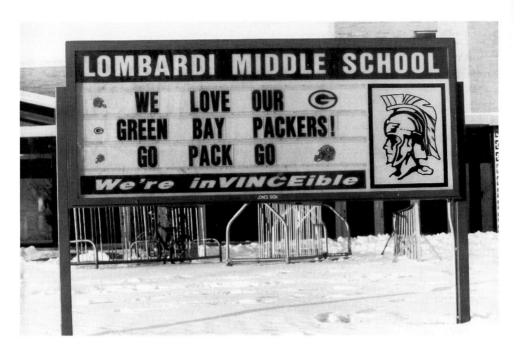

• At the school named after their old coach,
Fuzzy Thurston and Jerry Kramer visit junior cheeseheads.

* A vintage car by a vaunted stadium bears a vanity plate.

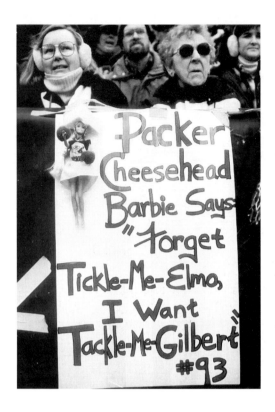

Packer fans come in every age, gender, and race...

...wearing cheeseheads and bratheads, beads and bows.

• The ghosts of Lambeau Field: Bart Starr salutes…

...Max McGee broadcasts, and Fuzzy Thurston cheers.

* Willie Davis embraces the past (Paul Hornung) and the present (Reggie White).

• In the locker room, Don Beebe faces a microphone and Frank Winters ponders a backgammon move.

• Desmond Howard makes the special teams special.

• Dorsey Levens and Edgar Bennett
share the running chores.

• Coach Holmgren points, Eugene Robinson watches, and Reggie White rejoices.

• Paul Hornung raises his arms but decides to leave
the Lambeau Leap to the younger Packers.

• The Pack's back.

Limbaugh. Imagine an *offensive* broadcaster named
Rush Limbaugh.)

Michels started nine of the Packers' next eleven
games. He sat out the San Francisco game with a knee
injury—Brown filled in—and then the following
game, against Tampa Bay, he shared playing time with
Ruettgers, who had finally decided to test his knee, to
play despite chronic pain, despite a degenerative condition.

Ruettgers reclaimed his place in the starting lineup
three weeks later, against Dallas, and did not play
badly. The coaches, in fact, were delighted with his performance and his condition, but Ruettgers himself did
not share their delight. He decided that the pain was
too great, too restrictive. With five games left in the
regular season, with the Super Bowl in sight, Ruettgers
announced his retirement.

"I made the decision myself," Ruettgers says. "I
struggled with it for several weeks. I didn't even talk to
my wife about it until the night before. It was a decision I had to make myself. Pulling the trigger was
heartbreak. All the years and all the work and all the
commitment."

Packer fans wrote to Ruettgers, thanking him for his
contributions to the team, and Edgar Bennett sent him
a fruit basket, Sean Jones a bottle of champagne. "At
least I was part of this season," Ruettgers says. "I just
couldn't finish it."

Bruce Wilkerson finished the season at left tackle, in
his tenth NFL campaign, his first with the Packers. The
305-pound veteran started the final game against Min-

nesota, supplanting Michels, and earned the job for the playoffs. The coaches suggested that the six-foot-seven Michels, who had lost weight during the season, down from 290 pounds to a feathery 270 or 275, had grown weaker. "He's got to get stronger," Tom Lovat, the line coach, said.

Michels could have protested or pouted, but, instead, he said and did the right things, the unselfish things. "We're all competitors here," he said. "We all want to be starters. But first and foremost I want this team to win. I understand and respect the coaches' decision.

"Bruce Wilkerson has been in this league for ten years. I can learn so much from him."

Mike Holmgren couldn't have phrased it better himself.

On first and ten from his own 32-yard line, 68 yards away from the end zone, Bart Starr passed to Donny Anderson for 6 yards. On the next play, Chuck Mercein ran for 7 yards and a first down. Starr connected with Boyd Dowler once, with Anderson twice, and the Packers had a first down on the Dallas 30-yard line with a minute and a half to play. Chuck Mercein gained the next 27 yards in two plays. He caught a pass for 19 yards and ran for 8. The Packers were 2 yards from a first down, 3 yards from the end zone, with less than a minute to play. Mercein had gained 34 yards in the dramatic drive.

"Every athlete's dream is to have the opportunity to perform," Chuck Mercein told me twenty-nine years later, "especially to perform in a spotlight. I was doubly blessed. I got the opportunity, in the brightest spotlight, and I was able to perform. That was the defining moment of my career, and it came in the defining moment of an unforgettable game."

Mercein, a Yale man, was in a sense the Andre Rison of the 1967 Packers, less heralded but equally valuable. A journeyman at best in a brief NFL career, discarded by the New York Giants, then placed on the practice squad, the "taxi squad," by the Washington Redskins, Mercein was available when Packer running backs started going down in 1967 the way their receivers went down in 1996. He was brought in to replace Elijah Pitts.

In 1996, Mercein joined the Packers who had played in Super Bowl I and Super Bowl II on Alumni Weekend in Green Bay. "I'm proud that I was able to contribute to that great, great team," Mercein said, "and those players, they're still appreciative. They told me, 'Chuck, you were a big part of that last drive.' "

It was the first time Mercein had been in Green Bay since the days following the Ice Bowl.

Anderson gained 2 yards, reached the Dallas 1-yard line, first down and goal to go with thirty seconds to play. Anderson crashed into the right side of the line and got nowhere, stopped at the line of scrimmage. The Packers called timeout with twenty seconds left, then tried the same play, and this time Anderson slipped on the frozen field and skidded to the 1-foot line. Timeout. Third and goal. Sixteen seconds to play. Still 17–14.

Willie Davis focused on Reggie White. "You try not to measure yourself against him," Davis says, "but you can't help thinking, *Gee, would I have made that play? Would I have gotten there?*"

How would Davis's Packers have done against White's Packers?

Willie smiles, aware that his view is biased. "I haven't seen a team yet that somehow we wouldn't have beaten," he says.

Davis also studied the crowd. "They're a special breed," he says. "I thought of all the fans over the years who had asked me when the Pack would be back."

Brett Favre once again picked up a first down on a quarterback sneak in the fourth quarter, setting up Chris Jacke's third field goal of the day, and then a pair of timely defensive plays, a Wayne Simmons sack and a Craig Newsome interception, killed a pair of Carolina drives.

The score was 30–13, but broadcaster Jim Irwin, determined not to jinx the Packers, said he wasn't quite ready to claim victory. His partner, Max McGee, had no such qualms. "Would you call Pat O'Brien's for me?" McGee said. "I think I need a hurricane."

The hurricane is the house specialty at Pat O'Brien's saloon in the French Quarter of New Orleans.

Willie Davis knew, too, that the game was effectively over, that the Packers were going to the Super Bowl.

"It was one of the great moments of my life," he says. Davis closed his eyes. "Every big play of the past seemed to come into full view in front of me," he says. "I saw Bart going into the end zone."

In the final minutes, Jim McMahon replaced Brett Favre at quarterback, and Bart Starr, in the comfort of a private box, stood and applauded, saluting Favre with a standing ovation.

Sixty thousand fans cheered as lustily, if not as knowledgeably, and Reggie White welcomed Favre to the sidelines with a huge hug. The good old boy from Mississippi whispered into the ear of the Baptist minister from Tennessee, "Congratulations, you deserve this," and joyful tears trickled down White's cheeks.

Brett Favre reminds me of the only other athlete from his high school, Hancock North Central, who went on to professional sports, a basketball player named Wendell Ladner. I covered the murder of three civil-rights workers in Philadelphia, Mississippi, in 1965, and from the day I had lunch with the local sheriff and his deputy, who were two of the men accused of the murders, I was wary of Mississippians. Until I met Wendell. Like Favre, he didn't seem to have a prejudiced bone in his body. When he played for the Nets in the American Basketball Association, Ladner shared a house in Long Island with a black teammate.

Wendell also went to the same college as Favre, Southern Mississippi. His coach, a legendary character named Babe McCarthy, once said of Ladner, "Wendell does not know the meaning of fear, or most other words."

Ladner laughed as heartily as anyone. He was a good old boy who died too young when his flight from New Orleans crashed trying to land in New York.

McMahon, perhaps the least devout member of the Packers, kneeled three times to end the game.
Green Bay 30, Carolina 13.

Lombardi could've sent in the field-goal team, could've gone for a tie, could've aimed for victory in overtime. Instead, with no timeouts remaining, the Packers went for the touchdown. In the huddle, Bart Starr said, "Thirty-one wedge, and I'll carry the ball." A quarterback sneak.

Starr took the snap and drove to his right, following Jerry Kramer and Ken Bowman, who lifted Jethro Pugh of the Cowboys, forced him slightly to his left, opened a hole just wide enough for Starr to bull through, to stretch and reach the end zone. Talk about tough. Starr wanted that touchdown.

Thirteen seconds later, the clock ran out on the Dallas Cowboys. The Packers won the Ice Bowl, 21–17.

The Packers' numbers against Carolina were awesome. They ran and passed for 479 yards, a Green Bay record for postseason play. Favre, after completing only two of his first eight passes, completed seventeen of his next twenty-one. Bennett rushed for 99 yards, and Levens amassed a total of 205 yards, 88 on ten rushes and 117 on five receptions, by far the best day of his young professional career. Levens gained only 46 yards less than the entire Carolina team.

"They belong in New Orleans," said the Panthers' Sam Mills, who was in on fourteen tackles, but, like Lamar Lathon and Kevin Greene, did not sack Favre even once. "We belong in Charlotte."

The Packer defense was no less impressive. Carolina picked up only 45 yards rushing, and in the first half, when the outcome was still uncertain, the Panthers managed merely 13 yards on the ground, their longest run a meager 4 yards. Gilbert Brown, the main weapon against the run, deserved a medal, or at least a meal. "Gilbert Brown is a load in the middle," John Madden told the world.

Gilbert Brown blossomed in 1996, literally and figuratively. At the start of the season, he was listed at 325 pounds, but then local Burger Kings began offering a Gilbert Brown burger, a double Whopper with double meat, double cheese, double mayo, double everything, except pickles. Gilbert doesn't eat pickles. Nobody ate more Gilbertburgers than Gilbert himself. Often he stayed late after practice, putting in extra time in the training room, which kept him down to 350, or 360, late in the season. Remarkably, Brown was a sprinter in high school. He was rumored to be capable of running the forty in 4.8 seconds. He may be the world's fastest 350-pound human.

"How strong is Gilbert?" says his line coach, Larry Brooks. "I very seldom see two guys move him. You're looking at six hundred and something trying to move three hundred and something, and they don't move him very far."

The special teams, the kick-return teams and the kick-coverage teams, did their job, too. Desmond Howard's 49-yard kickoff return was the most visible contribution, but hardly the only one. Travis Jervey, a second-year player from The Citadel, made the tackle on three Packer kickoffs. Jervey got downfield fast.

Mark Chmura may be the strongest of the Packers—he once bench-pressed 315 pounds nineteen times in a row—but Travis Jervey is the fastest, faster even than Don Beebe. Jervey placed fourth in the NFL's 1996 fastest-man competition. He was the only white player in the race and, at 225 pounds, outweighed the next heaviest sprinter by close to 40 pounds.

During his rookie year, Travis and his Packer roommate bought a lion cub for a pet. The cub grew quickly, and even though Jervey could outrun him, Mike Holmgren suggested that the lion be donated to the Green Bay zoo. Jervey complied.

The coach does believe in pets. He himself has two dogs, a pug, which can be traced back to China, and a cockapoo, which can be traced back to the coupling of a cocker spaniel and a poodle.

The coach does not believe in risky hobbies. He would like Jervey to donate his surfboard to a zoo, too.

Jervey and Chmura are fierce rivals for the designation of "Prettiest Packer," Caucasian division. Jervey gets extra points for being single, Chmura a bonus for being a starter.

By beating Carolina, the Packers improved their all-time record in postseason play to nineteen victories and eight defeats. No other team in the NFL has won more than 70 percent of its playoff games.

Carolina's fans were treated far more kindly in Green Bay than Carolina's football team. "As we stepped off the bus at Lambeau Field, it was not the cold that overwhelmed us but the warmth of the Packer fans," Hal Brown of Charlotte wrote to the *Press-Gazette*. "We were greeted with friendly smiles and handshakes everywhere we went . . . offered hot cocoa and handwarmers by the Packer fans who surrounded us . . . We hope to see many of you for the game here in Charlotte next year. We will do our best to match your Northern hospitality. Go Pack Go."

"People would . . . invite us to their tailgate parties, make sure we had handwarmers and blankets," another Charlotte fan, Michael Raus, wrote. "You fans are what football is supposed to be."

"San Francisco spat on us, Jacksonville spat and cursed, and Dallas was rude," Jeri Chandler wrote from Charlotte, "but Green Bay wrapped us in warmth before and after the game. . . . One friend . . . thought he might have frostbite. Packer fans around him removed his boots, took two plastic bags and filled them with their own handwarmers and wrapped his feet in the bags. . . . We left feeling a kinship with the Packer fans and will be rooting for you in the Super Bowl."

Not all Packer fans, however, are candidates for sainthood. Early in the season, when San Francisco's Bill Walsh stopped to sign autographs, he accidentally handed a 49ers playbook to a Green Bay couple, who passed it along to the Packers. The *Press-Gazette* gave the zealous fans the kind of heroic exposure New York newspapers and television stations gave the twelve-year-old boy whose interference with a fly ball at Yankee Stadium may have cost the Baltimore Orioles a home run in the 1996 American League Championship Series.

And when Minnesota came to Green Bay for the last game of the regular season, a woman who looked to be in her seventies or eighties proudly wore a sweatshirt that said: VIKINGS SUCK.

After the dramatic ending to the Ice Bowl, fans poured onto the playing field, descended upon the goal posts and savaged them, carted away scraps for souvenirs, almost as if they knew the memories would have to last them for decades.

The Packers warned their fans that they would not be permitted on the field at the conclusion of the Carolina game, that the goal posts were not to be violated, that anyone trespassing on the field was subject to a fine of $650 or more. Lieutenant Bill Parins, the head of Lambeau security for the Green Bay Police Department, and Jerry Parins, the Packers' corporate security officer and a former Green Bay police lieutenant, were both committed to keeping the field clear. They were cousins, Bill and Jerry, both related to the Honorable Robert J. Parins, the former judge who preceded Bob Harlan as president of the team. Green Bay really is a small city.

The new sheriff of Brown County was also on hand.

When Tom Hinz was twenty-four years old, safely home from the war in Vietnam, he went to the Ice Bowl. He went to patrol sections eight and ten near the north end zone.

Hinz was a rookie Green Bay cop then. Twenty-nine years later, he was the assistant chief of police. He decided to run for sheriff of Brown County in 1996 and, as a last-minute write-in candidate, won the Republican nomination. He anticipated a difficult race against the incumbent, Mike Donart, a Democrat.

But Donart committed a strategic error. When critics suggested that he should be replaced because some inmates had recently escaped from the county jail, Donart responded by running a newspaper ad showing Reggie White in his Packer uniform and asking:

"If he missed one tackle, would you trade him? It's a ridiculous thought, isn't it? Yet that is exactly what some people are suggesting we do with Brown County Sheriff Mike Donart."

Reggie White was not amused. He did not know

Donart, and Donart had not asked his permission to use his name or picture. White said the ad was unethical. He also said he hoped Hinz would win.

Reggie did know Hinz. The assistant police chief of Green Bay doubled as a bodyguard for Mike Holmgren on Packer road trips.

The *Press-Gazette* took Reggie's side and, in an editorial, assailed Donart's ethics. Hinz won the election handily, by 40,000 votes out of 90,000 cast, and in a cartoon, the newspaper gave White much of the credit. The cartoon showed Reggie standing over a flattened Donart and saying, "Gee, another sack. I guess *my* job's still secure."

The inmates who escaped probably deserved to get at least an assist on the sack.

Green Bay's loyal and obedient fans behaved perfectly, stayed off the field, figuratively and perhaps literally frozen to their seats as they watched the postgame ceremony, the presentation of the Halas Trophy to the NFC champion. Virginia McCaskey, George Halas's daughter, presented the trophy to Bob Harlan, who accepted, aiming a dart at Dallas, on behalf of the "real America's team."

Harlan said, "This is for the greatest fans in the world," and Reggie White, echoing his words, told those fans, "I hope you're proud of us because we're proud of you."

"We're gonna go down to New Orleans and we're going to win the Super Bowl for Green Bay," Sean Jones added.

Keith Jackson was less ebullient. "I'll tell you one thing," he said. "It's still cold."

Halfway across the country, at his home in Seattle, Washington, Vince Lombardi Jr. sat in his TV room and listened to the postgame comments and grinned with pleasure. Vince had stopped being much of a football fan several years earlier. He had grown tired of hearing about the Packers and the glory days and Vince Lombardi Sr. When he was reminded of his father's greatness, he was reminded, too, of his father's sternness and aloofness, and of the gulf that had widened between them. He envied the old Packers. They were, in some ways, closer to his father than he was.

"I don't know why people would assume I'd be jumping up and down when the Packers beat Carolina," Vince told me, "but goldingit, I really got excited. I was touched: White and Jones and Robinson, a bunch of black guys telling sixty thousand white people that they did it for them. I think that's good for the country. I really got a kick out of it. I got a whole lot more worked up and excited than I ever thought I'd be."

Vince Lombardi Jr. had another thought. "I was thinking to myself," he said, *"I'm gonna be so happy if they win it all 'cause then all those poor people in Green Bay can stop walking around saying the greatest thing that ever happened in their lives happened thirty years ago."*

As the temperature hovered above zero, Mayor McCrory of Charlotte, North Carolina, stood on the new sod of Lambeau Field and performed the Packar-ena. He was paying off a bet he had made with the mayor of Green Bay.

The victory over Carolina was a major milestone in the checkered history of Green Bay, a history that went back to the Pottawatomies, the Winnebagoes, the Menominees, the Osaukee, even a few Kickapoos and some Fox and Sauk, the tribe whose Oklahoma branch spawned one of the pioneer players of the National Football League, Jim Thorpe.

The French were the first Europeans to settle the area, drawn by the fur trade. (John Jacob Astor later owned the Green Bay Company, a fur-trading giant, but, as far as anyone knows, never set a silk-stockinged foot in the town.) The first Belgian, Father Louis Hennepin, showed up in 1675, but for 175 years, his countrymen resisted following him. Then, in the middle of the nineteenth century, when they heard that land was available at $1.25 an acre, thousands of Belgians made the pilgrimage to Wisconsin. Curly Lambeau was of Belgian descent; Mayor Jadin was of Belgian descent; Dr. Julius Bellin, who begat Bellin Hospital, was of Belgian descent. A strip of land 20 miles wide and 50 miles long, stretching from Green Bay to Sturgeon Bay, became home to the largest concentration of Belgians in the United States. (Which makes it doubly disappointing that, unless steak or whitefish thrills you, the restaurants in Green Bay today are remarkably unremarkable. Mayor Jadin, true to his Belgian breeding, says it is one of his ambitions to upgrade the local cuisine.)

In the mid–nineteenth century, Fort Howard, on the west side of the Fox River, and Green Bay, on the east, were incorporated as separate cities, but in 1895, after almost half a century of rivalry, the two voted to merge. By 1900, Green Bay was a metropolis of 18,684 people, many of them involved in the paper business, which was nourished by the Fox River Valley. By 1923, Green Bay, its population doubled, was the world's leading producer of toilet paper, and the world's largest distributing center for cheese.

By then, prohibition had descended upon the United States, and Green Bay was one of the country's major violators. In 1928, the Feds raided the area and padlocked fifty-one speakeasies. But by the next year sin was again flourishing. The *Milwaukee Journal*, in a two-part series detailing the decadence of Green Bay in 1929, reported that, "Wine, women and song are all to be had in variety." Which may have made it easier to recruit the players who brought the Packers three straight NFL championships in 1929, 1930, and 1931. Prohibition ended in 1933, and, probably only coincidentally, the Packers suffered the only losing season in the first three decades of their existence.

By 1959, the dawn of the Lombardi era, more than 60,000 people lived in Green Bay; by 1992, when Mike Holmgren showed up, the population was close to 100,000. In 1996, when Green Bay was the 210th largest city in the United States and the eight-story Bellin

Building was the tallest structure in town, *Forbes* magazine reported that Green Bay was the eighth fastest-growing city in the country in terms of producing jobs, *Money* magazine reported that Green Bay was the eighteenth safest city in the country and Packerland Packing, the largest beef packer east of the Mississippi, reported $1 billion in sales. "And some people think that we're nothing but igloos," Mayor Jadin says.

Jerry Kramer was among the spectators with connections who were guided onto the field after the game. He saw his young friend, Aaron Taylor, and hugged him and said, "Helluva game, helluva game."

Taylor beamed and said, "We're going all the way," and Kramer said, "You betcha ass you are!"

Kramer said "you," not "we," careful not to intrude on a new generation's glory.

As the celebration progressed, as the Packers began to realize that they were the NFC champions, they were going to the Super Bowl, they had to deal with conflicting emotions. They were euphoric because they had earned the Green Bay Packers' most significant victory in twenty-nine years, in their own stadium, in front of 60,000 deliriously happy fans. But the euphoria was tempered by the realization that the season was not over, that they still hadn't reached the summit, that they still had to scale the Super Bowl, and that if they didn't, if they stumbled, then the victory over Carolina—the whole season, in fact—would seem tainted and hollow.

* * *

As the celebration tapered off, two fans, Ann LaForce and her husband Dave Petry, asked a policeman for permission to slip into the south end zone just for a minute so that they could scatter the ashes of Ann's father, Ed LaForce. The policeman obligingly turned his back. Ed LaForce had died more than two years earlier. His daughter had been waiting for the proper hallowed moment.

Mike Holmgren's speech after the NFC championship game started predictably. "Men," he said, "I am proud of you." He also told his players, once again, that it had been a long season, that they had beaten a good football team, that they had won because they had played unselfishly. But then, in the middle of his talk, Holmgren choked up for the first time all season.

"You have to enjoy the journey," he said. "You have to enjoy the road to get there. You've worked too hard—all of us have worked too hard—not to enjoy every moment. Now this is a special moment." Holmgren paused and fought back tears. The players, kneeling around him, cheered him on. "Let it go, baby," they called. "Let it go!"

Holmgren caught his breath and resumed. "Go out tonight," he said. "Have a good time. Celebrate. But be smart."

Then the players bowed their heads and recited The Lord's Prayer in unison. When the prayer was done, Keith Jackson lifted his eyes and said, "Who we?"

"Packers!" his teammates responded in unison.

"Who we?" Jackson repeated.

"Packers!"

"Who we?"

"Packers! Ooooooh!" And the team broke up in cheers and laughter and hugs, as proud of their immense cleverness as their major victory.

Willie Davis could not leave without stopping in the locker room. "I just want to say," he told Reggie White, "you guys are a great football team."

"Hey, thank you, man," White said. "I really appreciate it."

Paul Hornung, the honorary co-captain, came to the locker room and hugged the winning coach. "It was neat," Mike Holmgren said.

"Everyone expected us to win this game today, including ourselves," Brett Favre said, "and we did. I'm assuming everyone will pick us to win the Super Bowl. But anything can happen."

Jerry Kramer, his son Tony, and his son-in-law Scott Magnus made the post-game pilgrimage to Shenanigans. As they entered, Fuzzy's customers began to chant, "Jer-ry, Jer-ry, Jer-ry!" And then: "Hall of Fame! Hall of Fame! Hall of Fame!"

"It was feel-good time," Kramer said.

As Reggie White left the locker room, he spotted Brett Favre. The minister and the recovering addict embraced again, and White said, "Where are we going tonight?"

"Oh, we're going partying tonight," Favre said, and the two men laughed.

That night, Brett Favre joined Frank Winters and Aaron Taylor at Mark Chmura's house with a few friends, including Hootie & The Blowfish and David Spade of *Saturday Night Live*. Just a typical Sunday evening at home in Green Bay.

BOOK TWO

EXORCISING THE GHOSTS

Green Bay vs. New England

January 26, 1997

Super Bowl XXXI would not have been nearly so super without the Green Bay Packers. The tradition they represented and the town they represented, one almost infinite, the other almost infinitesimal, were both legendary. Green Bay and football went together, like New England and chowder.

The New England Patriots were "the other team," the opponents, the underdogs, the supporting cast. The only tradition they brought to the game was one of chaos. In the thirty-seven seasons of their existence, the Patriots had changed their name once and their home often.

As the Boston Patriots, they played their home games at four different ballparks: Boston University Field, Harvard Stadium, Fenway Park, and Boston College Alumni Stadium; as the New England Patriots, they played their home games at Schaefer Stadium, Sullivan Stadium, and Foxboro Stadium, three different names for the same structure, situated south of Boston in a town called Foxboro.

They had even more head coaches than home fields, thirteen in all, with the average tenure several games short of three seasons. One of the coaches who brought down the average was Phil Bengtson, Lombardi's assistant and immediate successor in Green Bay; Bengtson lasted exactly five games in New England.

The Patriots had one distinction: They played their games in a smaller city than the Packers did. Foxboro's official population was 16,044. The odds were that the team would change its name to the Foxboro Patriots shortly after the Dallas Cowboys became the Irving Cowboys, and the New York Giants the East Rutherford Giants.

No matter what name they used, where they played or under whom they played, the Patriots had never won the championship of the NFL or the AFL. And only one man who played the bulk of his career with the Patriots had earned a place in the Pro Football Hall of Fame: John Hannah, an offensive guard whose hero, and role model, was Jerry Kramer.

The Patriots had gone to the Super Bowl once, in 1986, and had been beaten by what was then the widest margin in Super Bowl history, thirty-six points. The Chicago Bears, led by Jim McMahon, who passed for 260 yards and ran for two touchdowns, an MVP performance even if he didn't get the award, crushed New England, 46–10.

The Patriots had a history about as rich as snow-boarding's.

The lone Patriot who brought exceptional football credentials to New Orleans was the head coach, Bill Parcells, who had won two Super Bowls, XXI and XXV, when he coached the New York Giants. His career could be traced back, in a way, to Green Bay's glory days. There were far fewer than six degrees of separation between Vince Lombardi and Bill Parcells.

One of Parcells's college teammates at Wichita State, Bob Long, played for the Packers in Super Bowls I and II. While Long wore green and gold, Parcells served, as Lombardi once had, as an assistant coach at West Point. Parcells went on, like Lombardi, to be an assistant with the Giants. The links with Lombardi went all the way back to Parcells's high school days—his high school coach, Mickey Corcoran, played for Lombardi at Saint Cecilia's High School—and even further. Growing up in Oradell, New Jersey, one of Parcells's sandlot-football playmates was Vince Lombardi Jr. "I could've been rooting for Parcells to win the Super Bowl," Vince Jr. says, "but I wasn't."

With all his ties to the Lombardi family, Parcells could've been rooting for the Packers to win the Super Bowl. But he wasn't.

Bob Long was. "But don't tell Parcells," he says.

In their junior year in college, Parcells and Long worked together at a pizzeria on the edge of the Wichita State campus. The pizzeria was the country's first

Pizza Hut. Parcells was then a tackle and linebacker on the football team, Long strictly a basketball player. Long suggested that Parcells work in the kitchen, on the ovens, which required moving only a few feet side to side, like a tackle, and that he, Long, work in the dining room, serving the pizzas, which, of course, required the greater dexterity and quickness of a shooting guard.

The next fall, Long went out for football for the first time. He played in only seven games, but set five Wichita State pass-catching records. He and Parcells were both drafted, Long in the fourth round by Green Bay, Parcells in the seventh by Detroit.

Parcells, the football player, didn't make it.

Long, the basketball player, shared in three championships in Green Bay and, before he concluded a successful seven-year career, rejoined Lombardi for a season in Washington.

Parcells went into coaching, and Long into Pizza Huts. Eventually, he owned thirty in Wisconsin. He persuaded Max McGee to invest $2,000 in Pizza Hut, which grew to $250,000 and enabled Max to launch ChiChi's, the chain that made him, like Long, a millionaire.

Recovered from a stroke that temporarily affected his speech and balance, Long is now the president of the NFL alumni association in Wisconsin. He elected not to go to New Orleans, but to watch Super Bowl XXXI at home in front of the fireplace.

A decade earlier, Long did go to Super Bowl XXI, in

Pasadena, to see his college teammate and Hutmate, Bill Parcells, coach the Giants to the championship.

Mike Holmgren had never been the head coach of a Super Bowl team, but he was no stranger to the atmosphere. Twice, he went to Super Bowls as the offensive coordinator of the San Francisco 49ers, and both times, in 1989 against Cincinnati and in 1990 against Denver, Holmgren saw his team, led by Joe Montana, win the game. Holmgren could match Parcells, ring for ring.

"Savor the moment," he told his players the day after the NFC Championship game, thirteen days before the Super Bowl. He reminded them how many great players—O. J. Simpson, for one; Merlin Olsen, for another—had never played in a Super Bowl.

Seven of Holmgren's Packers were going to their first Super Bowl after playing ten or more seasons in the NFL. Five of them were starters: Reggie White, Sean Jones, Eugene Robinson, Bruce Wilkerson, and Frank Winters. Mike Prior and Jeff Dellenbach were reserves.

Holmgren also advised his players to take care of family travel and ticket arrangements early in the week so that they could concentrate on the New England Patriots for the rest of the week. Each player was told he would be able to acquire thirty tickets, two free, the rest at face value, at $275 apiece. The players, of course, planned to use all their tickets for friends and family, as long as you consider ticket scalpers and travel agencies to be friends or family.

Holmgren made the decision to coach as if the Super

Bowl were being played Sunday, January 19, instead of Sunday, January 26. He was going to treat the off week as if it were the game week: Watching films on Monday, off on Tuesday, full workouts on Wednesday, Thursday, and Friday and a light workout on Saturday before flying to Louisiana on Sunday. Holmgren's thinking was that once the Packers arrived in New Orleans all the demands and distractions of Super Bowl Week would interfere with normal preparations, would have an impact on workouts and meetings. He wanted the Packers to be prepared early.

"We're not going down there to party," Frank Winters said. "We're going down to win a championship."

For a day, the Super Bowl was the most important thing in the world to Frank Winters. Then he received a phone call from his family in New Jersey. His brother John, two years older than Frank, had died of congestive heart failure. Suddenly, the Super Bowl didn't seem quite so consuming. When someone commented on the unfortunate timing, Winters said, "There's no good time for this."

He made arrangements to leave the team for two days, to go home for his brother's funeral. "We've got a strong family," Winters said. "We'll get through this."

Midway through the off week, Mike Holmgren asked his two Super Bowl veterans, Don Beebe and Jim McMahon, to address the team, to tell them what to expect in the days leading up to the game. Their areas of expertise, of course, did not overlap.

Beebe was the expert on generic Super Bowls. He had been to four of them, in Tampa, Pasadena, Atlanta, and Minneapolis.

McMahon was the expert on New Orleans Super Bowls. His only Super Bowl game was played in the Superdome.

Beebe's most famous Super Bowl moment was his pursuit of Leon Lett.

McMahon's most famous Super Bowl moment was his pursuit of baser pleasures.

McMahon was accused during Super Bowl XX of insulting the intelligence of the men of New Orleans and the morals of the women. He denied he said the women of the Big Easy were easy, but he did admit to baring his bottom to a television news helicopter. He also admitted that he knew where Bourbon Street was.

"It's the little bad angel, and the little good one," Mike Holmgren said, as he presented McMahon and Beebe to their teammates. No one raised his hand to ask which was which.

Sean Jones phrased it more harshly. "It's the Christian and the anti-Christ," he suggested.

Beebe told his teammates to avoid distractions.

McMahon told them where they were.

"He told us not to get arrested," said the rookie, John Michels.

The Packers did have another authority on Bourbon Street on their roster. Brett Favre had no experience in a Super Bowl, but plenty in the French Quarter. He grew up perhaps an hour away, and New Orleans was the closest cultural center.

Before the Packers left Green Bay, Favre was asked if Holmgren had counseled him on how to behave in New Orleans. "What could he tell me?" Favre said. "Watch this? Watch that? Stay off Bourbon Street? I know what I've got to do. It's the biggest game I've ever played in. I'm not going to screw it up."

Favre smiled. "If this was three years ago," he admitted, "maybe Mike would have had to room with me."

Favre conceded that he was anxious to go south, to see his family and to see the sun. He was packed and ready to leave by the middle of the week. "I can't wait," he said. "It's like a thousand degrees below zero here. I'm calling home every day and asking, 'What's it like outside?' and my mom says, 'It's pretty cold right now. It's like fifty-eight.'

"I'm coming off that plane in sandals, T-shirt, and my hat on backward."

The Green Bay Packers, like the New England Patriots, were allotted 17½ percent of the seats in the Superdome, some 12,600 tickets. Which meant that no more than one out of every five season ticketholders was lucky enough to be a winner in the Packer lottery, earning the opportunity to purchase a ticket to the Super Bowl at $275 apiece.

Some who missed out placed classified ads in the

Press-Gazette, seeking—*begging for*—tickets. One ad offered two 1997 season tickets in exchange for two Super Bowl tickets; another offered two weeks in a high-rent vacation home on Lake Michigan in return for a Superdome pair.

Packer fans willingly paid scalpers $1,000 or more for a seat in the end zone; tickets at the 50-yard line commanded as much as $2,500, a princely sum in a workingman's town. Of course if you averaged it out over twenty-nine years, it didn't seem quite so expensive.

Thousands of fans who couldn't buy, beg, or barter tickets made plans to go to New Orleans anyway to soak up the atmosphere and the brews, to help transform Bourbon Street into Lombardi Avenue for a few days. They pounced on $1,000 tour packages, "bargain" rates for a charter flight and four nights of economy lodging, nothing more. Some intended to watch the game on television only a few blocks from the Superdome; others planned to make pilgrimages to Mississippi to view the game in the Broke Spoke, the only tavern in Brett Favre's hometown. It was like going to Boston to watch the final episode of *Cheers*, or to Dallas to find out who shot J.R.

As temperatures in northeastern Wisconsin dipped toward zero, and below, more and more Packer fans figured out ways and excuses to head south, to temperatures reported to be in the fifties and sixties, equatorial heat by Green Bay standards. Even the ghosts headed toward the Gulf. Fourteen of the men who suited up for one or both of the first two Super Bowls made plans to spend Super Bowl Week in Louisiana, the state in which Willie Davis and Jimmy Taylor and Lionel Aldridge and Bob Brown were born, and Max McGee went to college.

Three of the Super Bowl XXXI Packers—Santana Dotson, Doug Evans, and Shannon Clavelle—were also born in Louisiana, obviously a fertile football state. And Brett Favre was born just the other side of the border.

As soon as New England won the AFC Championship game, the oddsmakers established the Packers as twelve-to-thirteen point favorites to win the Super Bowl. Within a few days, the price rose to fourteen points. Holmgren, naturally, said the spread, the largest since Baltimore was favored to beat the New York Jets by eighteen points in Super Bowl III, was ridiculous. He reminded everyone that the Jets upset the Colts.

There were similarities between the Patriots and the Jets. Each had the best record in its division, but not in its conference. Each had a young quarterback in the fourth season of what promised to be a magnificent career. And each had a veteran coach with a history of success in championship games. But:

Weeb Ewbank and Joe Namath had a far better supporting cast than Bill Parcells and Drew Bledsoe had.

Brett Favre was much closer to his peak at twenty-seven than Baltimore's Johnny Unitas was at thirty-five.

Favre had a better supporting cast than Unitas had.

The NFC champions had beaten the AFC champions in twelve straight Super Bowls.

The NFC champions had won those twelve games by an average of twenty-one points.

The New England Patriots had lost to the Denver Broncos, the only team in the AFC with a record better than theirs, by four touchdowns, 34–8.

The Green Bay Packers had defeated the Denver Broncos, the only team in the NFL with a record as good as theirs, by five touchdowns, 41–6.

The Packers deserved to be favored by fourteen points.

At least.

The Packers may not have been one of the greatest teams in NFL history—they were neither so explosive offensively as, say, the 1983 Washington Redskins, nor so stingy defensively as the 1986 Chicago Bears—but they were certainly one of the best balanced. The 1983 Redskins were not among the top defensive teams, the 1986 Bears not among the top offensive teams, which may explain why neither won the Super Bowl. The Packers excelled both ways.

One measure of the Packers' balance was that only two of their players, Favre on offense and Butler on defense, were named to the All-Pro team. Dallas and Denver, neither of whom reached the conference finals, placed four men apiece. Only Reggie White and Keith Jackson were selected to join Favre and Butler in the Pro Bowl (Frank Winters was added later, to replace an injured center); nine Cowboys were chosen for the game, and seven Broncos. However, Dallas, offensively, and Denver, defensively, had noticeable weaknesses. Green Bay did not.

One week before Super Bowl XXXI, the Packers flew from a wind-chilled 35 below to a sunny 65 above, a swing of roughly 100 degrees. A couple of hundred Packer fans waited at the New Orleans airport and cheered, "Go, Pack, go," when Brett Favre stepped off the plane in sandals, T-shirt, and sunglasses, and his hat on backward. Jeans and a light sweater were his only concession to the wintry weather he had left behind.

Jim McMahon is a hero to Brett Favre. Brett admires how knowledgeable McMahon is about football. He also admires how nonchalant McMahon is about football, or, as Brett puts it, "He doesn't give a shit about anything."

With as much awe as envy, Favre says, "He comes to meetings hung over. And then he talks during the meetings."

"I've never pretended to take football seriously," McMahon says. "I don't think the game is that hard. It's like chess. You're trying to outmaneuver the other team, expose the weaknesses you see.

"I've had some great coaching over the years, especially in college. I played for three different offensive coordinators who eventually became head coaches.

I've tried to pick people's brains and find things out.

"But to me, it's not that hard. I don't worry about defensive lines and linebackers. That's the other guys' job, the guys up front and the backs. My job is to find out what the secondary is doing and whether or not my protection is good for what's coming. It's not very hard."

"He'll be watching the films," Favre says, "and he'll go, 'Oh, shit, that's not going to work.' He knows. Instantly."

"Brett's never been schooled in the passing game," McMahon says. "Up until he got to the pros, he said he'd never gotten into a seven-on-seven drill, which is just a skeleton drill where you're throwing the ball. I was doing that in high school in California."

Does Favre remind him of himself?

"A little bit," McMahon says. "He plays the game the way it's supposed to be played. You've got to play to win. He's a tough kid. He plays hurt. He's got a lot of confidence in himself. Yeah, he reminds me of myself a bit."

Favre and Holmgren both think of McMahon as sort of an unofficial coach.

"That sucks," McMahon says. "I'd rather be a player."

McMahon is remarkably likable for a man who works so hard at being unlikable.

For the first seven years of his NFL career, McMahon was intensely disliked in Green Bay. He was, as much as Walter Payton, the personification of the hated Chicago Bears. "Packer fans didn't like me and I didn't like them," McMahon admits.

McMahon has never much liked the media, either, with some justification, but when he has deigned to talk to reporters, he has almost always provided colorful copy. In the twilight of his career, he describes himself as "the designated false-chatter man," clapping and chirping on the sidelines, full of phony rah-rah.

One of the annual rituals for Packer players is picking out a local youngster the first week of training camp at Saint Norbert's College in De Pere, one of Green Bay's neighboring communities, and borrowing his bike every day to ride back and forth to the practice field. The kid runs along next to the player, carrying his helmet. At the end of the exhibition season, the player generally gives the youngster a gift, a pair of practice gloves or a pair of used cleats. The kids, naturally, love the bond with the athletes; Packer fans by birth, they become Packer fans for life.

McMahon didn't borrow a bicycle. He rode his own motor scooter back and forth to the practice field.

The kids loved him, anyway. He was wearing the right uniform now.

As the result of a car accident before his final college season, Brett Favre had part of his intestines removed, and as a result of the surgery, he is subject to massive buildups of gas. Favre loves to share these buildups with his friends and teammates. He also takes pleasure in hiding and detonating truly horrendous stink bombs in the locker room. Sometimes his teammates have difficulty distinguishing the stink bombs from the quarterback. He disgusts them on both counts. Sean Jones and others have threatened his life. They forgive him mostly because he has a great arm.

Early in Super Bowl Week, a New Orleans cab driver started telling his passengers how tough the quarterback for the Green Bay Packers was. "He can throw with two guys hanging on him," the cab driver said.

"If two guys are hanging on him, he must not get much blocking," said Brett Favre, who was one of the passengers.

The other two passengers, Mark Chmura and Frank Winters, winced.

A fine writer and reporter, Peter King of *Sports Illustrated*, asked Brett Favre during Super Bowl Week his thoughts about fame, and Favre's reply was both honest and wise. "It's been everything I ever dreamed it would be," he said, "and more. But there's a downside, a side you don't see when you're growing up and wishing you could be on TV and in the papers all the time, and that's your private life. There is no private life. You can't go out with your family. You can't go out and walk the streets. Sometimes I wish I could change my identity. But I enjoy fame. It means that I'm playing football, and doing well, and that's what I've always wanted to do."

* * *

Their cab took the three Packers to Hooters, which also attracted a few of their teammates and a few of their opponents. New England's Dave Richards, a veteran lineman who talked a lot and played little, invited himself to join Favre, Chmura, and Winters. He began telling them how hard Bill Parcells pushed the Patriots. "We're working in full pads tomorrow," Richards said.

"We haven't worked in full pads since midseason," said Winters. "Our workouts are mostly mental."

Favre drank to that. He had a Diet Pepsi.

Richards also mentioned that Parcells had set no curfew for the Patriots; Holmgren enforced a 1 A.M. curfew for his players.

"One of our guys never came back Monday night," Richards said. "He missed the bus to the Superdome Tuesday morning. He still hadn't showed up."

Favre drank another Diet Pepsi.

Favre was gracious to well-wishers and autograph seekers, relaxed, not the least resentful that his friends drank beer while he drank soda pop. He laughed at the incongruity of it. "I never thought I would spend seven days in New Orleans and not be out partying," he said. But he wasn't feeling sorry for himself. "Way more than a million people," he said, "would like to be sitting where I am now. They'd love to be staying in a nice hotel, preparing for this game. That's all I have to remember." Favre paused. "We could easily have lost the NFC championship game and then we'd be partying like everyone else. I've been to this town a million times. I love it. It's a great city. But I'll have plenty of time to come back here and enjoy myself."

Jerry Kramer arrived in New Orleans a few days before the game, accompanied by his four sons. The older two grew up in Green Bay, during and after the glory days; the younger two were still growing up in Idaho, both football players, one at the University of Idaho, Jerry's alma mater, the other at Parma High School. Jerry wanted them to share the excitement of the Super Bowl, the camaraderie of his old teammates, and, of course, the joy of his election to the Pro Football of Fame.

He had been a finalist before, and had been disappointed, shut out despite glowing credentials. Kramer had made the Associated Press All-Pro team five times in the 1960s; he was one of four Packers who were named to the NFL's All-50-Year team in 1970, the fiftieth anniversary of the league (the other three—Cal Hubbard, Don Hutson, and Ray Nitschke—had all been inducted into the Hall many years earlier). Besides his blocking, besides his part in leading the Green Bay sweep, Kramer had kicked three field goals to lift Lombardi's Packers to the 16–7 victory over the Giants that gave them their second NFL championship.

In the quarter of a century that the Seniors Committee had been recommending inductees, the majority had been accepted, but several—Mac Speedie and Willie Galimore, for instance—had been turned down.

The late Henry Jordan, Kramer's former teammate and neighbor, had been rejected in 1989, then elected in 1995.

Based on the Seniors Committee's nomination, Kramer's bid would be voted on by the full National Board of Selectors, thirty-six active or former sports reporters and columnists. Thirty of the Board members represented each of the NFL's thirty cities; five were at-large choices and one represented the Professional Football Writers Association of America. Thirty affirmative votes were required for election; seven no's and you're out.

Twelve of Kramer's Green Bay contemporaries, including Emlen Tunnell and Vince Lombardi, had already been inducted. Some people felt that was too many Packers. Some of the people who felt that way were on the Board of Selectors.

Reggie White called Brett Favre often in the two weeks after the NFC championship game to remind him that the Super Bowl was coming up. Brett assured Reggie that he hadn't forgotten. He also remembered that they were playing New England.

Reggie did not want to take any chances on losing the Super Bowl. If it had been up to him, the Packers would have all gone to sleep by nine-thirty each night during the week leading up to the game.

Keith Jackson could hardly wait for game day. "I feel like a thirty-five-year-old woman who hasn't had a child," he said. His biological clock was ticking.

*   *   *

"Even though this is what you've been waiting for your entire life," Brett Favre said, "you can't wait for it to be over."

Edgar Bennett remembered that when he was a kid, he would watch the Super Bowl on television and then run outside to play football and announce, "I'm Tony Dorsett," or, "I'm Franco Harris," depending on who won. "I guess there'll be some kids who'll be us this Sunday," he said. He hoped so.

One of the more bizarre sights on Bourbon Street, which has more than its share, was Ray Nitschke pushing a baby carriage, cooing to his granddaughter wrapped in pink.

Larry Brooks, the Packers' defensive line coach, spotted Nitschke and said hello. Nitschke told him how impressed he was by Brooks' front four. "It must start here," Nitschke said, jabbing Brooks with his finger.

Brooks was delighted. "It's a great compliment," he said, "coming from a guy who played like he did."

Jeff Thomason, the Packers' third tight end, arrived in New Orleans by a circuitous route. He came into the NFL in 1992 as a free agent and spent two seasons with the Cincinnati Bengals, catching a pass almost as rarely as the Bengals won a game. In 1994, in training camp, he was cut by the Bengals and then by the Packers. He gave up football for a year and took up skiing.

In 1995, still in one piece, he went back to Green Bay

and made the team as a backup tight end, first behind Chmura, then, after Keith Jackson signed, behind Chmura and Jackson. Early in the 1995 season until he was injured, the Packers carried another tight end, Mike Bartrum, whose background was strikingly similar to Thomason's. Bartrum, too, began his NFL life as a free agent; he was signed by Kansas City, which threw to him even less frequently than the Bengals threw to Thomason. Bartrum, too, was cut in training camp in 1994, spent a season away from football, then won a spot on the Packers, largely for his long-snapping skills.

Thomason and Bartrum were roommates in the Packers' training camp in 1996, friends and rivals, well aware that, with Chmura and Jackson both healthy and under contract, only one of them would be kept. Thomason won the competition; Bartrum became expendable.

The two tight ends were reunited in New Orleans, still friends and still rivals. Bartrum was in town to play in the Super Bowl, for the New England Patriots.

Ron Wolf had traded Bartrum to the Patriots for "past considerations," which means, essentially, that he was a gift to Wolf's old friend, Bill Parcells. He was a useful gift. He served as the Patriots' long-snapper on punts, extra points, and field goals, and he caught a pass for the first time in his professional career. It was his only reception all season, and it was only for 1 yard, but it went for a touchdown.

When Jeff Thomason heard about Bartrum's touchdown, he cheered. Thomason hoped that someday he, too, would score a touchdown in the NFL.

They met for drinks in the French Quarter, Thomason and Bartrum, two men who were out of football in 1994 and in the Super Bowl two seasons later.

The city of Las Cruces, New Mexico, announced that it would celebrate Super Bowl Sunday, January 26, as Darius Holland Day. Holland, who went to high school in Las Cruces, was a backup tackle for the Packers. If he were a starter, the whole state probably would have celebrated Darius Holland Day.

All through the week, the Packers did what Super Bowl teams are supposed to do: They said nothing but kind words about their opponents. They praised Drew Bledsoe's arm and Terry Glenn's legs, Bill Parcells' brain and Willie McGinest's brawn. They made each Patriot sound no less formidable than such ex–New Englanders as Ted Williams, Bobby Orr, and Larry Bird. They did not believe every word they said.

"I'm tired of saying how great this team is," Wayne Simmons told his Green Bay teammates. "I've been watching them on film, and they look like crap."

Bonita and Irvin Favre, the parents of Brett, sat on stools at the bar in Molly's-on-the-Market, a New Orleans saloon just a long pass away from the Mississippi River. Irv, crew-cut, short, and stocky, looks like Central Casting for a drill instructor. He was his son's coach in high school. Bonita Favre is a sturdy and attractive woman. Irv ordered a beer. Bonita asked for sex-on-the-beach.

The so-called "celebrity bartender," a Super Bowl custom in Molly's, did a double-take. He had never heard of sex-on-the-beach. Not the drink, anyway. Bonita Favre explained that it was a blend of peach schnapps, Southern Comfort, and grapefruit juice. Sounded terrific. The celebrity bartender awkwardly concocted the drink.

Bonita Favre gulped it down.

Irv Favre sucked on his beer.

I was the so-called celebrity bartender. I tried one of each.

Tom Brown, the former safety, came to New Orleans to sell nostalgia, literally, to be part of the memorabilia wing of the NFL Experience, a floating interactive theme park featuring tests of football skills, historical displays, and of course, merchandise for sale. Brown was selling Lombardi lithographs to raise money for Tom Brown's Rookie League, a nonprofit program dedicated to teaching children to enjoy sports. "I sold prints to people from California, West Virginia, Florida," Brown says. "It was amazing how many of them remembered the sixties."

Willie Davis thought the old Packers would have figured out a way to beat the new Packers.

Lionel Aldridge, the other old defensive end, thought there was no way. The new Packers were too big, too fast, and too strong.

Want to bet?

You could—in Las Vegas.

The oddsmakers established the Super Bowl I Packers as three-point favorites over the Super Bowl XXXI Packers.

Meaning that if you wanted to bet on the new Packers to exceed the old Packers' thirty-five points in Super Bowl I, you would get three points. If you wanted to bet on the old Packers, you had to give three points.

You could also bet on the quarterbacks head-to-head. Bart Starr threw for 250 yards in Super Bowl I, and the wizards of odds said Brett Favre was even money to match him.

Starr and Favre were even in many ways. Bart played in his first NFL championship game in his fifth season, and lost. Brett played in his first NFC championship game in his fifth season, and lost. Bart won his first NFL title in his sixth season. Brett won his first NFC title in his sixth season.

Bart Starr had the highest postseason rating of any quarterback in NFL history, 104.8. Brett Favre had the fourth-highest, 93.5.

If Brett Favre had not made it to Super Bowl XXXI, if he had not been able to go from a painful defeat in the NFC championship game in Dallas to an exhilarating victory in the NFC championship game at Lambeau one year later, he would have had so many excuses—the death of his friend, the troubles of his brother and sister, the six-and-a-half weeks of rehab, the stress of withdrawal and abstinence, the pressure of retaining his Most Valuable Player status, the pounding he endured without painkillers. But he made it. "I've always found a way to beat adversity," he said.

"So many good things happened, and so many bad things," he said. "Maybe the bad things helped me focus. When I was on the field, I escaped from everything else. I put all my energy into football."

Through the tragedies and trials, Favre never even thought of giving up. "Not once did I doubt myself," he said.

A few minutes after noon the day before Super Bowl XXXI, Jerry Kramer heard the results of the Hall of Fame balloting. The owner Wellington Mara, the coach Don Shula, the defensive back Mike Haynes, and the center Mike Webster were elected. Kramer was not. He did not wince. Not visibly. He hid his feelings.

His teammates did not.

"I was shocked and hurt," Herb Adderley said. "I was flabbergasted. I told my girlfriend, and she couldn't believe it, either."

"I thought he was a shoo-in," Tom Brown said. "I thought it was automatic. I can't believe anyone didn't vote for him."

"I was devastated," Willie Davis said. "I was so sure it was going to happen. It took all the fun out of my day."

"Paul and Bart and Jimmy are in the Hall of Fame," Fuzzy Thurston said. "Somebody must have blocked for them."

In the afternoon, Jerry Kramer and Willie Davis, once roommates and still friends, encountered each other on Bourbon Street and embraced. Willie almost cried for Jerry, who smiled and signed autograph after autograph for the Packer fans flooding the sleazy street, outnumbering Patriot fans by a huge margin.

New Orleans had been transformed into Wisconsin South. People from Ashwaubenon and De Pere bumped into friends and neighbors in the French Quarter. The Pack came marching in, Mardi Gras beads dangling on green-and-gold jerseys bearing Brett's number 4 or Reggie's number 92. It was a marriage of true minds, the cheeseheads and the Big Easy. Health agencies reported that New Orleans had the highest per capita rate of obesity of any city in the country; Wisconsin had the highest rate of obesity of any state. Cheese and beer bellied up to po' boys and andouille.

Twenty-four hours before the game, one Green Bay fan announced that, no matter how much fun she was having, she was pulling out of New Orleans, flying home to suit up her cats. "If I don't," Mary Ann Miller of Beaver Dam, Wisconsin, explained, "the team won't win." The day of the Kansas City game, she had trusted a baby-sitter/cat-sitter to dress the cats in their "game" jerseys, number 4 and number 92. The sitter, instead, had put on their numberless "practice" jerseys. "That's why we lost," Mary Ann said. She certainly wasn't going to trust the Super Bowl to a stand-in.

*   *   *

Mike Holmgren presided, as always, over the Saturday night meeting of the Packer offense, unveiling his script for the first fifteen plays of the game, a practice pioneered by his mentor, Bill Walsh. Sherman Lewis, the offensive coordinator, and the offensive assistants made suggestions, but Holmgren, who had been both a quarterback coach and offensive coordinator in San Francisco, wrote the final draft.

Holmgren had perhaps a thousand plays to choose from, all of them stored on computer, many offering only slight variations on a basic theme, a change in formation, a change in blocking assignments, a change in pass routes. For each game, Holmgren and his assistants try to limit their arsenal to no more than a hundred passing plays, no more than twenty-five running plays, choosing, naturally, the ones that would tend to work best against the anticipated defenses. Most teams focus on fewer plays. "We do it a little differently," Holmgren says. "We don't repeat much. That's a philosophy we have."

For the Super Bowl, he decided to start off with relatively simple, risk-free plays, designed to help Brett Favre build his confidence, help him ease into the flow of the game mentally and physically. Favre had started erratically in the previous post-season games—completing one of his first three passes against San Francisco, two of his first eight against Carolina—and Holmgren didn't want that to happen again in the Super Bowl.

For the first fifteen plays against New England, Holmgren chose nine throws and six runs. The first play was Edgar Bennett off tackle, an ultra-safe selection: Between his rookie season and the 1996 season, Bennett rushed 726 times without fumbling the ball away. The second play was a short pass, 5 or 6 yards, called 322 Y Stick, a quick out to Mark Chmura. "A very high percentage throw for us," Holmgren says. "We complete about ninety percent of those to the tight end."

The offense digested the plays, the team digested a snack of sandwiches and fruit, and curfew was at 11:00 P.M.

On the eve of Super Bowl XXXI, Max McGee told people he was going to stay out all night in New Orleans just to prove he could *broadcast* without sleep. McGee had proved he could *play* without sleep in Super Bowl I. The night before that game, which he was expecting to watch from the bench, he had snuck out after curfew to resume acquaintances with a blond young woman he had met only a few hours earlier. McGee had returned to the Packers' hotel roughly in time for breakfast.

When Boyd Dowler was injured on the second play of Super Bowl I, Max McGee replaced him. Starr promptly passed to McGee. "It was a little quick turnout," Max recalls, "and I turned, and the ball was on me so quick it hit me in the helmet. Went through my hands and—bong! I said to myself, 'Boy, this is gonna be a great day, right?'" It was the greatest day of McGee's long career. He caught seven passes—three more than he had caught in the entire regular season—for 138 yards and two touchdowns.

Jim McMahon was one of the few new Packers old enough to have watched the old Packers play. "I used to love the Packers," he says. "Who didn't? Bart Starr and all those guys, they were on top. Everyone loves a winner. They were great players. They were fun to watch. I love the Max McGee stories. The Super Bowl stories.

"From what I know and what I've heard, Max had a good time with his life. But when it came time to play, he played. What you do off the field is insignificant. It's what you do on the field that counts."

McGee had lost a step by 1997. At midnight the night before the Packers met the Patriots, Paul Hornung told me he was sorry, but he had to leave my Super Bowl party to take Max home and put him to bed. "It's past his bedtime," Hornung said. Then he smiled. "Mine, too," he said.

Before Brett Favre went to sleep the night before the Super Bowl, he reviewed the game plan and realized that he and his coach were actually thinking alike. "A couple of years earlier," Favre says, "we didn't think that was possible. We're different in lots of ways, and our philosophy of football may be a little different. But we both want the same thing, we both hate to lose and we both believe that hard work is going to get us there."

*   *   *

The churches of Green Bay were ecumenically be-hind the Packers on the morning of Super Bowl XXXI. Parishioners at Saints Peter and Paul Catholic Church showed up for 9 A.M. Mass wearing Packers colors, matching the green and gold of the priests' vestments. Outside the First United Church of Christ, a sign spread the gospel: For God so loved the Packers He sent Reggie.

Six hours before game time, people lined up outside Shenanigans, waiting to get in to watch the game on television, wanting to be able to say that they stood and drank elbow-to-elbow with Packer fans in a bar owned by one of Lombardi's people. Hotel rooms were as coveted in Green Bay as they were in New Orleans; all 3,100 rooms in Brown County sold out. The big difference was that you didn't have to take the room in Green Bay for four nights, and you didn't have to pay $250 a night or more.

Fuzzy Thurston was not at Shenanigans. He was having breakfast at Brennan's, the New Orleans land-mark, with Paul Hornung, who was getting ready to leave town. Hornung had a speech scheduled the next day in Florida, and he wasn't able to get a reservation on a Monday-morning flight. He would fly out Sunday afternoon and get to his Florida hotel room before the Super Bowl ended.

Hornung was one of four old Packers who left New Orleans before the kickoff. Tom Brown went to Statesboro, Georgia, to watch the game with his son, a base-ball player at Georgia Southern; Jimmy Taylor headed to Illinois, to host a Super Bowl gathering for a gambling casino; and Boyd Dowler, who had been one of three old Packers participating in the Taste of the NFL, a food-and-wine-tasting festival, returned to his home in Tampa.

(The Taste of the NFL, which raised money for the hungry and homeless, paired a chef from each NFL city with a player representing the city's team. Dowler represented Tampa Bay, his hometown team; Chuck Mercein represented the New York Giants, his original team; and Fuzzy Thurston represented the Packers. The Green Bay chef came from a restaurant called Smokin' Joe's Southern Grill, which serves a variety of Cajun dishes, including a tasty gumbo. Only Green Bay would be bold enough to send a chef to cook Cajun food in New Orleans, the heart of Cajun cuisine. The chef's name was Shel Gorzelanczyk; he was probably not of Cajun origin.)

Eleven men from Super Bowls I and II remained in New Orleans to attend XXXI in person: Donny Anderson, Tommy Joe Crutcher, Willie Davis, Jerry Kramer, Max McGee, Chuck Mercein, Ray Nitschke, Dave Robinson, Bob Skoronski, Bart Starr, and Fuzzy Thurston. Not a bad lineup, bolstered by Ron Kostelnik's widow, Peggy, and Elijah Pitts's son, Ron.

Elijah Pitts, the son of an Arkansas sharecropper, the father of a network broadcaster, scored two touchdowns in Super Bowl I, the first breaking open a 14–10 game, the second wrapping up a 35–10 victory over the Kansas City Chiefs. Elijah, who came out of an obscure Little Rock college called Philander Smith, was in his sixth season as a Packer, his first as a regular, sharing the running chores with Jimmy Taylor, who scored his final Green Bay touchdown in Super Bowl I.

Almost three hours before game time, the Packers boarded the buses that would take them from their headquarters, the Fairmont Hotel, to the Superdome barely half a mile away. Every player wore a tie and a jacket except one. Brett Favre wore his favorite uniform, shorts, sandals, and short-sleeved shirt.

In the ballroom of the Trump Plaza hotel in Atlantic City, Herb Adderley, the former Packer; Ben Davidson, the former Raider; Jim Marshall, the former Viking; and Roman Gabriel, the former Ram, were the celebrity hosts of a Super Bowl party. All except Gabriel had played in Super Bowls, but only Adderley on the winning side. Adderley played in four Super Bowls and won three, the first two with the Packers, the third with the Cowboys.

Jim Marshall also played in four Super Bowls, but lost all four, all with the Minnesota Vikings, the bridesmaids of the seventies. "I'll never get over the hurt," Marshall said. "I don't go to football games because of that."

Before the game began, each of the former players was asked which team he thought would win, and why. Adderley's opinion carried extra clout because, during the three-hour pregame show on Fox, he was one of five Packers named to John Madden's all-time All-Madden Super Bowl team. Willie Wood, Willie Davis, Ray Nitschke, and Jerry Kramer were also named; Kramer was the only Packer on the offensive team. The coach of the All-Madden team was, of course, Vince Lombardi. All of the honored Packers were in the Pro Football Hall of Fame, except one.

Adderley picked the Packers to beat New England, he said, "Because they have the best defense in the league, and they can control the ball."

Willie Wood was in Palm Springs, California, the guest of a pharmaceutical company that was delighted to have a former Super Bowl star mingling with its clients as they sat in bleacher seats in a large auditorium and watched Super Bowl XXXI on a giant screen. The bleachers were divided into a blue section for Patriot fans, and a green section for Packer fans. Wood perched in the green section, rooting for his old team, coached by his fellow Southern Cal quarterback. "I was just hoping that they'd play as well as I thought they could play," Wood said.

Marv Fleming was also watching the game in a fashionable California neighborhood, at a friend's house in Bel Air. Fleming dressed for the occasion. He wore a cheesehead, a gift from thoughtful friends in Wisconsin. "I was very fortunate to be a Green Bay Packer," Fleming said.

* * *

Some of the Packers were understandably tense in the locker room before the game. Brian Williams threw up for fifteen minutes. Jim McMahon, as usual, broke the tension. He stood at one end of the locker room and began throwing passes at the nameplates above the individual stalls. On his first three throws, he knocked off three nameplates, matching his completions for the season. To celebrate, McMahon demonstrated the end-zone dance that he said he would perform if he scored a touchdown.

His teammates fell on the floor laughing.

White men can't dance.

Reggie White went into the Super Bowl with dreadful postseason statistics by his own special standards. He had made only three tackles in two games, had assisted on none, and did not have a sack, a forced fumble, or a fumble recovery to his credit. Of course, no one knew how many times his presence had persuaded opponents to run to the opposite side of the field.

White did go into the game with extra incentive. He said that Bill Parcells had deprived him of two Super Bowls. The New York Giants could have selected White with the third choice in the 1985 draft of players from the folding United States Football League, but Parcells passed on White and picked an offensive lineman. Philadelphia took Reggie with the next choice. Parcells's Giants won two Super Bowls in the next six seasons while White watched enviously.

*   *   *

Bart Starr shared a luxury box in the Superdome with a group that included a few bankers, his former teammate Donny Anderson, and his fellow quarterback Dan Marino. Marino had played in Super Bowl XIX, in only his second NFL season, and even though he had lost, to Joe Montana and the 49ers, he had not been particularly discouraged. He had fully expected to win at least one Super Bowl, and probably more, before he finished his career.

Now it was twelve years later, as he watched the Packers and the Patriots, and Marino had never returned to a Super Bowl, except as a spectator. He owned almost all the important NFL passing records—most completions, most passing yardage, most touchdown passes, all the records Brett Favre was taking aim at— but Dan Marino didn't own a Super Bowl ring. And at the age of thirty-five, the odds were against him.

Bart Starr completed sixteen of twenty-three passes in Super Bowl I for 250 yards and two touchdowns. He permitted one interception. Most Valuable Player in the NFL in the 1966 season, he was also MVP in Super Bowl I.

"This is it," Mike Holmgren told his players. "This is what you've been working for. You guys are the best team in football."

Andre Rison was moved, partly by the words, mostly by the occasion. He began to cry.

Sue and Fuzzy Thurston entered the Superdome and looked at each other. "Oh my God," Sue Thurston said.

"We're here." When Luther Vandross sang "The Star Spangled Banner," Fuzzy was moved. He began to cry.

No one was happier than Fuzzy that the Packers were in the Super Bowl, not even Reggie White. No one wanted them to win so badly, not even Brett Favre.

Fuzzy Thurston was the only old Packer who was born and raised in Wisconsin.

Jeff Dellenbach started the 1996 season with the New England Patriots and was released after the first game. At the age of thirty-three, after eleven years as an offensive lineman in the NFL, the first ten with the Miami Dolphins, Dellenbach feared his career was over. It was—for three months. In December, he signed as a backup center and long-snapper with the Green Bay Packers.

Dellenbach was the only new Packer who was born and raised in Wisconsin.

Green Bay came out blazing on three fronts: Special teams, defense, and offense. On the opening kickoff, Keith McKenzie, the rookie from Ball State, sliced through the Patriots' return unit and dropped Hason Graham at the 21-yard line. David Letterman must have been proud.

New England quickly tested its running game, and flunked. Curtis Martin, coming off a second straight 1,000-yard season, carried three times in the first two minutes and gained a total of 1 yard. Martin ran only four more times the rest of the first half.

New England punted, and again the Packers' special teams

delivered. Desmond Howard, delighted to see that the Patriots were not kicking away from him, demonstrated his delight by running away from them, a 32-yard return, sprung by a fine Bernardo Harris block, to Green Bay's 45-yard line.

Then the offense took over, briefly. On second and nine at the 46, after Edgar Bennett probed left tackle for a yard, Favre came to the line of scrimmage and saw that the Patriots had brought up both safeties to cover Green Bay's two tight ends, Mark Chmura and Keith Jackson. Favre recognized the defensive alignment from the videotapes he had studied. He figured the Patriots were going to blitz their linebackers.

In the morning, in his hotel room watching highlights of Super Bowl XXIV, Favre had seen Joe Montana, in a similar situation, call an audible, change the play.

"We didn't think it would happen that early in the game," Favre said, *"but I took a chance and checked to a maximum protection and gave Andre a chance to beat him to the post."*

In other words, Favre decided to forget about the short, high-percentage pass to the tight end. He audibled, changed the play from 322 Y Stick to 74 Razor, calling for Andre Rison to run a deep post pattern, to start down the left side, then break to the center of the field, toward the goal post. He also called for extra blocking, to give himself time to throw long to Rison.

Rison took off and sprinted 15 yards downfield, faked to the outside, then slanted to the inside. Otis Smith, the Patriots' cornerback, took the fake, turned the wrong way. When he realized his mistake, Smith had to twist to make a 180-degree turn. By then, Favre's perfect pass was leading Rison toward the end zone.

"I knew if I got the protection, he would beat his guy," Favre said.

Rison made the catch in full stride and, all by himself, a few yards from the end zone, began celebrating the brilliance of the 54-yard play with an exaggerated duck walk. The Packers had a 7–0 lead, and the game was only three-and-a-half minutes old. Mike Holmgren loved the way Favre had edited his script.

"I told him it was fine to audible, IF it worked," Holmgren said, *"and that one worked beautifully."*

Favre went slightly crazy. He raced to the sidelines, almost skipping, his helmet in his hand, a huge smile on his face. Favre, after putting up with questions all week about his slow starts against San Francisco and Carolina, was clearly ecstatic.

"I was just so excited," Favre said, *"that it turned out exactly the way we had practiced it."*

Dave Robinson, sitting next to his wife in the Superdome, went wild, too, cheering Rison's move. "It was so disciplined," Robinson said. "What made it so great was that it came from a guy people thought wasn't disciplined."

"I wasn't surprised," said Bart Starr, who had sent Favre a note during Super Bowl week, wishing him luck. "I didn't think New England could cover the Packer receivers."

As soon as Rison caught the ball, Herb Adderley said, he sensed the Packers were going to win big. In Atlantic City, he turned to his girlfriend and to Jim Marshall and said, "This is gonna be a long day for Otis Smith. He can't play the corner."

When Otis Smith was in Philadelphia, Adderley's hometown, the Eagles *hoped* he could play cornerback. "I talked to him many, many times," Adderley says. "He'd say, 'Give me a few pointers, Herb,' and I'd tell him, 'Be conscious of your field position. Know where the sidelines is, 'cause that's your best friend, that's your twelfth man.' Things like that. But he just couldn't adjust. Andre Rison gave him a little shake move and turned him around and that was it."

Willie Wood turned to the Patriot fans in the blue bleacher seats in Palm Springs and gloated, "The fat lady's started singing already."

"Gee, I hope it's not a rout," said Marv Fleming, rubbing his cheesehead. "I want to see the Packers win, but I want to see a good game."

The Patriots got the ball back for only two plays. On the first, Gilbert Brown nimbly dropped back into pass coverage—imagine Danny DeVito jumping center—and brought down the receiver, Curtis Martin, after only a 1-yard gain.

On the next play, Drew Bledsoe threw longer, but not more successfully. As the ball sailed downfield toward Shawn Jefferson, Doug Evans leaped in front and made a spectacular interception, juggling the ball, controlling it, and getting both feet down in bounds at New England's 28-yard line. Jerry Seinfeld must have been proud.

Two minutes later, Chris Jacke kicked a 37-yard field goal, and Green Bay led 10–0, and the first quarter wasn't even half over. The Packers were awesome. The Patriots were gruesome. The NFL record for one-sidedness—Chicago 73, Washington 0 in the 1941 championship game—probably wasn't in jeopardy. But the record for a Super Bowl rout—San Francisco 55, Denver 10 in 1990—was.

And then the game turned around.

On New England's third possession, Bledsoe threw seven passes in a row. Four of them were incomplete, but the first two completions, a pair of screens to Keith Byars and Curtis Martin, gained 52 yards, and an interference call against Craig Newsome, his first all season, gave the Patriots another 26. On a play-action pass from the 1-yard line, Bledsoe hit Byars, who once was Reggie White's and Keith Jackson's teammate in Philadelphia, for a touchdown.

The Patriots scored again before the first quarter came to a close, a short touchdown pass to Ben Coates set up by a 44-yard pass to rookie Terry Glenn.

Glenn's leaping catch came directly in front of Dave Robinson. "That was probably the greatest catch I've ever seen live," Robinson said.

Suddenly, the Packers were in trouble. "Enough is enough!" Fritz Shurmur screamed at the defense. "Pull your head out of your ass and do what you're supposed to do."

Not only were the Packers trailing, 14–10, but on three consecutive series, they went three-and-out, their longest gain 5 yards. Favre went two for six during the stretch. He was no longer jumping up and down.

But Favre wasn't worried, wasn't even discouraged. After the third straight fruitless possession, he met on the sidelines with his three main wide receivers, Freeman, Rison, and Beebe, all of whom said they were getting open. Favre said they were bound to come up with a big play.

The next time the Packers got the ball, first and ten on their own 19, they lined up with three wide receivers, Rison to the left, Beebe and Freeman to the right, outside the tight end, Chmura. Beebe was split wide, Freeman in the slot. A cornerback, Ty Law, faced Beebe. A rookie safety, Lawyer Milloy, faced Freeman.

"I started licking my chops when I saw that safety come up," Freeman said.

"It was kind of odd that they would put him on Free," said Favre.

"I knew that all I had to do was make him stumble or move the wrong way," Freeman said.

Milloy was supposed to bump Freeman, slow him down. He never laid a glove on him. Freeman took off.

"We send four guys up the field, and you just pick whoever," said Favre. *"I took the mismatch."*

"Everything got cloudy," was Lawyer Milloy's summation.

Favre threw a strike, right into Freeman's arms, and Free

flew toward the end zone. Milloy and the Patriots' other safety, Willie Clay, chased him, vainly.

"Once I caught the ball," Freeman said, *"all I thought about was quieting all the critics who said I wasn't fast enough when I came out of college, who said I didn't have the heart to go across the middle. I knew the whole world was watching and it was my opportunity to quiet those critics."*

The play covered 81 yards, the longest touchdown pass or run in Super Bowl history. The Packers regained the lead, 17–14.

"I ran like I have never run before," Freeman said.

A 62-yard touchdown pass, Bart Starr to Boyd Dowler, gave Green Bay a 13–0 lead over Oakland early in the second quarter of Super Bowl II. It was the longest touchdown pass or run in the first four Super Bowls.

Before the 1995 draft, the Carolina Panthers asked their scout, Boyd Dowler, to look at tapes of Antonio Freeman at Virginia Tech. "I liked Freeman," Dowler says, "but, quite frankly, I didn't see him doing on tape what he does now—which is running away from people. He plays faster on the field than he did on tape."

Frank Winters looked up into the stands and was able to spot his parents. "I knew where they were sitting," he says. "It was real tough to see them." He thought about his brother. "Before the game, during the game, after the game," Winters says, "he was always there in my mind."

Fritz Shurmur didn't want to see New England bounce back again. "Go get Bledsoe," he told LeRoy Butler. "Do whatever it takes. I'll blitz you every play if I have to. Just get in his face. I want him to feel you and worry about where you are all the time."

The Patriots' next drive fizzled when, on third and nine, the Packers blitzed Butler, Brian Williams, and Wayne Simmons. Butler won the race to Bledsoe and, with one hand, pulled the quarterback down. Bledsoe had thrown twenty-one passes in the first eighteen minutes; the Packers, quick learners, were beginning to ignore his play-action fakes. They were going for him instead.

Wayne Simmons, the "buck" linebacker, in Packer terminology, the strongside linebacker, and Brian Williams, the "plugger," the weak-side linebacker, both came to Green Bay full of promise—Simmons, a first-round draft choice from Clemson in 1993, Williams, a third-round choice from Southern Cal two years later. But both were perceived to be wanting in dedication, and both were in danger of being dropped early in their careers.

In 1994, his second season, troubled by a sprained knee, Simmons started only one game and missed more tackles than he made. "They were ready to trade me," he says.

In 1995, his rookie season, troubled by a groin injury, Williams didn't start a game, didn't make a tackle except on special teams. Fritz Shurmur, the defensive coordinator, wanted to cut him.

Fortunately for the Packers, neither of the young linebackers was cut or traded. In 1995, Simmons started every game and capped a strong season with a remarkable playoff game in San Francisco: He had sixteen tackles, including a sack, and forced the fumble that produced the game's first touchdown. He emerged as a leader of the defense.

In 1996, Williams emerged as a football player. He stunned everyone, especially Shurmur, with a sensational training camp. He led the team in tackles and looked so solid Shurmur felt comfortable moving George Koonce from the outside to middle linebacker, making Koonce the quarterback of the defense and putting Williams in his old slot.

Simmons and Williams play opposite sides and display opposite personalities. Williams is quiet and shy, hardly a typical Texan; he used to play saxophone in a gospel quartet. Simmons is brash, a needler. He picks on Eugene Robinson's teeth, says, "I bet you could gnaw nuts with them." He even picks on Shurmur.

During a game, waiting for defensive signals, Simmons is liable to turn to the sidelines and shout, "Hey, Fritz, you better get the call in. Don't leave us out here hangin'. Hey, I'm talking to you."

"No one in the world can get away with doing that except Wayne," Robinson says. "We say that he's Fritz's son."

"He's clever," Shurmur says. "He breaks the tension."

"Fritz loves me," Simmons says.

The main reason Shurmur loves Simmons is that he makes plays.

Simmons is also a phrase maker. He taught Favre the phrase, "Shit be bringin' it, hoss."

"He's very creative," Shurmur says.

Simmons is the team storyteller, the team joker. He is also the team enforcer.

Going into the Super Bowl, Simmons and Williams led the Packers in postseason tackles, eleven apiece against San Francisco and Carolina. Simmons also had an interception and Williams a fumble recovery. They were living up to their promise.

The man in the middle of the Packer linebackers was Ron Cox, the only defensive starter in the Super Bowl who was not a regular during the regular season. Cox was an insurance policy that paid off handsomely.

Cox spent his first six seasons with the Chicago Bears, then celebrated his twenty-eighth birthday on March 29, 1996, by signing with the Green Bay Packers. Ron Wolf gave him a terrific birthday present, a contract for more than a million dollars a year, and both Wolf and Cox expected Cox to become the Packers' starting middle linebacker.

Brian Williams's sudden development, however, pushed George Koonce into the middle, and Cox onto the bench. Cox endeared himself to Shurmur and Holmgren by neither complaining nor shirking, and when Koonce tore an anterior cruciate ligament in his right knee in the opening playoff game against San Francisco, Cox stepped smartly into the lineup.

Cox is tough. He's killed eight bears. Not his former Chicago teammates. Real bears, ranging in size from four hundred to six hundred pounds, bigger than Gilbert Brown. He hunts bears with bow and arrow. "With a gun, it's too easy," he says. Cox's favorite prey are wild pigs. He likes them, he says, "because they charge you, instead of running away." His second favorite prey are running backs, for similar reasons.

Cox is the nephew of Willie Stargell, the Hall of Fame Pittsburgh Pirate baseball player. Stargell wielded a bat the way Cox wields a bow. "With a gun, it's too easy," Willie says.

George Koonce came out of East Carolina in 1991, drafted by no one, tried to make the Atlanta Falcons as a free agent and was discarded before the season began. He quickly built a reputation in the World League of American Football, the NFL's international road company, then found a home, a following, and a wife in Green Bay.

Koonce moved into the starting lineup in his rookie season and stayed there until he was injured three weeks before the Super Bowl. Green Bay fans loved to serenade him, "Kooooonce," every time he made a tackle, and one of them loved him so much she married him. He was leading the team in tackles when he got hurt.

He turned over his position to Ron Cox and his radio show to Eugene Robinson.

Koonce's son Bryan, who turned seven before the 1996 season, is a Dallas Cowboys fan. So is Reggie White's son and Brian Williams's mother. So much for America's "real" team.

Desmond Howard kick-started the Packers' next drive with a 34-yard punt return into Patriot territory, just one block shy of breaking free. The drive ended with Jacke's second field goal, opening a 20–14 lead.

At halftime of Super Bowl II, the Packers led Oakland, 16–7, and Don Chandler, with three field goals and an extra point, had scored 10 of Green Bay's 16 points. Chandler was playing the final game of a remarkable career: In twelve seasons, he had played in nine championship games, six with the New York Giants, three with the Packers. He was the only man in NFL history to kick a field goal of more than 50 yards and a punt of more than 90.

The Packer kickers in Super Bowl XXXI, the two men who shared the chores Don Chandler once handled alone, were, like most NFL kickers, a team within a team, joined together by their lonely and pressurized jobs. In the mornings, while their swifter and more massive teammates watched game tapes, Chris Jacke and Craig Hentrich went head to head at backgammon and video golf games.

Jacke, the place-kicker, was in his eighth Packer season, the only member of the squad, after Ruettgers's retirement, who had suffered through the two dreadful years that preceded Holmgren's arrival (the Packers lost seventeen of their last twenty-one games before Holmgren showed up). Hentrich, who punted and kicked off, was in his third Packer season; he joined the team in 1994 after being cut in training camp by the New York Jets. "You're always on the edge in this business," Hentrich says. "I know I can never let up because thousands of guys want my job."

With little fanfare, little national attention, Jacke had become the second highest scorer in Packer history, trailing only Don Hutson and only by three points, a single field goal. Of all the Packers, he was the closest to being a loner, the most distant from his teammates. Still, he insisted, "It's like a family unit here," possibly because he remembered the losing years when Packer players used to point fingers at each other, assigning blame. Kickers always get more than their share of blame; it makes up for their not hitting, or getting hit, very often.

Hentrich had the advantage of being a Notre Dame man, of having played in college with Aaron Taylor, Dorsey Levens, Lindsay Knapp, and Derrick Mayes. Like most of the other Notre Dame men, Hentrich found that Green Bay reminded him of South Bend, Indiana, in size, in mood, in its obsession with football and tradition. Imagine a college town without classes or degrees; that's Green Bay (except for the students at UW–Green Bay). "The town bleeds and sweats Green Bay Packer football," Hentrich says.

He respected Green Bay's traditions, but did not get caught up in them. He had no idea who Don Chandler was. Chandler probably didn't know who he was, either. Hentrich was one of the few Packers who could walk around Green Bay and, at least occasionally, not be recognized. A slender six-foot-three, mild in manner and appearance, neither his size nor his race indicated that he was a football player.

Both kickers are talented golfers. Hentrich, who shoots consistently in the low seventies, has worked as an assistant to a Green Bay golf pro during the off-season and is thinking about playing golf for a living after football. He already makes money on the golf course, when he plays with Jacke.

Hentrich has also played golf with Ray Nitschke. "Nitschke gives me a lot of crap about being a punter," Hentrich says. "He hates punters."

Bledsoe threw three passes in a row when New England got the ball back. The first was complete for a first down, the second was incomplete, and the third was intercepted by Mike Prior.

The Packers then marched 74 yards in nine plays and six minutes, the first sustained drive of the game. Dorsey Levens, almost as effective as he had been against Carolina, carried four times, gained 31 yards, giving him 51 for the half, plus three receptions. Favre circled left end for the final 2 yards himself. Green Bay led at the half, 27–14, a wider margin than Lombardi's Packers had enjoyed in Super Bowl I or II.

Seated among the press, CNN reporter James Lofton, once a Packer, once Don Beebe's tutor in Buffalo, did not cheer. But he did not hide his feelings. "What this team has done," he said, "for me personally and, I hope, for everyone who played in that chasm between the sixties and the nineties, is bridge the gap. It lets us all, everyone who put on a Green Bay uniform for an extended length of time, become champions."

With ZZ Topp, the Blues Brothers, and James Brown, the Godfather of Soul, not the King of Running Backs, entertaining the crowd, the halftime break was long enough for Fidel Castro to deliver a speech, for Jesse Jackson to offer a medley of his finest sermons. Mike Holmgren took about two minutes for his remarks. He asked his players to lock arms, symbolizing their unity, and as they kneeled around him, he said, "We have gotten this far by staying together, by being close. We only have thirty minutes of football left. We will win this thing if we stick together."

Thirty minutes of football—and what felt like hours of waiting for the game to resume. The players' routines were thrown off. They had ankles retaped. They meditated. They urinated. Jim McMahon ate a hot dog. The minutes ticked by slowly. No one seemed more anxious than Desmond Howard.

He sat at his locker, just inside the door, to the right, and he stared at the clock, at the floor, back to the clock. He kept asking how much longer till the team went back on the field. He definitely did not want to

miss even one play of the second half of the biggest
and best game of his life.

Paul Hornung reached his hotel room in Florida in
time to watch the second half of the Super Bowl. He
made himself comfortable, ordered a meal from room
service. Anything to drink? Water, Hornung said, just
water. His doctor had told him two weeks earlier that
he had an arrhythmia, an irregular heartbeat, a fairly
common and not terribly threatening ailment. Still,
Hornung ordered water. He wasn't taking any chances.

Of course, Hornung, who was once suspended by the
NFL for a season for gambling, had bet on the game.

On the Packers.

There is no street in Green Bay named after Hornung, not yet, but Hutson Road runs off Packerland
Drive, Isbell and Hinkle and Lambeau Streets run off
Hutson and Starr Court runs off Lambeau. White Oak
Terrace is in the neighborhood, and so is Brett Favre's
home ("It's so big," Brett says, apologetically, "there's
parts of it I haven't seen yet."), but that's probably just
coincidence. Hubbard Street is not far away.

Curly Lambeau, Cal Hubbard, Don Hutson, and
Clarke Hinkle were four of the first five Packers elected
to the Pro Football Hall of Fame. It's not hard to understand why they haven't named a boulevard after
the fifth, Johnny Blood.

(There is, however, a local beer named after him. You
can get a glass of Johnny Blood Red at Titletown Brew-
ery.)

"They'll probably name an alley after me," Mike Holmgren says.

After the interminable intermission, the Packers took the kickoff and, with William Henderson and Mark Chmura each making his first catch of the game, marched 38 yards in eight plays. They reached the New England 37-yard line, fourth down and one to go.

"Well, I'd say they punt the ball, that's my guess," Max McGee guessed on WTMJ.

Many of McGee's listeners agreed.

Mike Holmgren disagreed.

The Packers did not go into punt formation.

"I'm wrong," McGee said. "But you don't want to reignite the other team. That's my opinion."

Boyd Dowler, once an assistant coach in the NFL, now a scout, began yelling at his television set. "No," Dowler commanded, "you got to punt the ball."

Dorsey Levens took the handoff from Favre, started toward right tackle, then veered outside. Actually, he veered backward. New England's middle linebacker, Ted Johnson, nailed Levens for a 7-yard loss. The Patriots took possession near midfield.

"They didn't get it!" McGee said. "That was a bad call. You don't run across the backfield like that on short yardage. That's just a very bad call. I didn't like the call at all. I think I would have punted the ball."

"I had a problem with the call," Dowler said.

"I think they just reinvigorated a team that was ready to die," McGee said. "If they come out and score here, we're going to be in a dogfight."

Two of the Packer coaches were already in a dogfight, screaming at each other on the sidelines. Nolan Cromwell, the special teams coach, objected to Fritz Shurmur, the defensive coordinator, using Lamont Hollinquest, a special teams stalwart, at linebacker. The forty-one-year-old Cromwell and the sixty-four-year-old Shurmur had to be separated by players. Even functional families have squabbles.

New England did not score immediately. But after an exchange of punts, the Patriots again took possession near midfield. A pair of Bledsoe completions brought them to the Green Bay 26-yard line, and then Martin, held in check all day, limited to barely 2 yards a carry, suddenly broke out, went off tackle for 8 yards, then up the middle for 18 yards and a touchdown. Gilbert Brown, known as "The Grave Digger," didn't bury Martin. Brown missed the tackle; so did half the Packer secondary. Green Bay 27, New England 21. The Patriots were reinvigorated. The Packers were in a dogfight.

"I was not feeling good," Dowler said.

"I got a little nervous," said Willie Wood.

Then the Patriots made a mistake: They kicked off.

They kicked off toward Desmond Howard. He took the ball on the 1-yard line. The Packers had called a "middle return": the Patriots anticipated a "sideline return." The mismatch worked perfectly for Green Bay. The Patriots cheated toward the sidelines, and the Packer wedge—Jeff Thomason, Lindsay Knapp, Lamont Hollinquest, and Keith McKenzie—helped them along. Open sesame! Open seam!

"I just tried to hit the hole at full tilt," Howard said.

Howard burst through the wedge, then followed Don Beebe toward the left sideline.

"I saw how big the hole was," Beebe said, *"and I said, 'We're going to score.' All I had to do was get on the safety, put my helmet in his pads, and then it's Desmond and the kicker, and there's no way the kicker's going to tackle him in the open field. Impossible!"*

When Desmond Howard reached midfield, Willie Wood's nervousness subsided in Palm Springs. "Bye-bye," Wood yelled. "Bye-bye."

Howard went 99 yards, a Super Bowl record, for the touchdown. He sprinted the first 95 yards and strutted the last four. He pranced in the end zone.

"That broke our backs," New England's Willie Clay said.

"That cut our heart out," his teammate, Keith Byars, added.

The Patriots were hurting everywhere.

"I knew that sooner or later I was going to scorch them," Desmond Howard said.

The pain multiplied when Favre and friend, Brett and Mark Chmura, teamed up for a two-point conversion, widening the Packers' lead to a full fourteen points, 35-21, with three minutes remaining in the third quarter.

"I was elated," Herb Adderley said.

In the fourth quarter of Super Bowl II, Herb Adderley intercepted a Daryle Lamonica pass and returned it 60 yards for a touchdown, still the second longest interception return in Super Bowl history. Green Bay beat Oakland, 33–14.

Howard's teammates were ecstatic.

"Desmond's the man," Gilbert Brown said.

"We love watching him," Brett Favre said.

"I was joking with him before the game," Dorsey Levens said. *" 'Don't take every kick back. Let the offense get a couple of reps in.' "*

"Brett Favre was, of course, the league MVP, and his numbers prove that," Sean Jones said. *"But if we had to pick a team MVP, it had to be Desmond. Any time he catches the ball, he can make so many special things happen."*

The older Packers, the ones in the stands and in front of the television sets, were ecstatic, too—about the first 95 yards of Howard's return. Most of them had reservations about his finishing flourish.

Chuck Mercein, one of the heroes of the 1967 NFL

championship game, was sitting behind the end zone, the end zone in which both Howard and Rison celebrated their Superdome touchdowns. "They both came at me," Mercein said, "doing that showboating stuff. It kind of made me cringe."

"I hate it," said Tom Brown, one of the heroes of the 1966 NFL championship game. "It has to stop. Desmond. Rison. All that damn dancing. Lombardi would turn over in his grave and have a heart attack."

Maybe not quite as good a line as the more classic version, "If Vince Lombardi were alive today, he'd turn over in his grave." But close.

"I work with young girls and boys," Brown continued, "and it filters all the way down to them. Everybody has to come up with a new dance."

"Vince wouldn't have gone for that dancing," Tommy Joe Crutcher said. "I'd rather not see it."

Crutcher is a country boy. One of his favorite expressions when he played in Green Bay was, "Ef a frog had wings, it wouldn't whomp its ass every time it jumped."

He was asked if he knew what "Shit be bringin' it, hoss" meant. Tommy Joe said he didn't have the slightest idea.

Jerry Kramer's initial instinct, too, was to shudder when he saw the extravagant end-zone displays. "A lot of people want everything to be like it was in the old days," he said. "They want everyone just to hand the ball to the referee and behave the way the old Packers did."

Kramer shook his head. "That's asking too much," he said. "These kids, they're thinking about their peer group and their buddies watching them at home and the other teams watching them, and they're having fun, that's all, and what the hell, that's okay. That's okay with me."

Desmond Howard was not nearly so demonstrative when he scored in college, for the University of Michigan, except once, the time he returned a punt for a touchdown against Ohio State and promptly lobbied for the Heisman Trophy by striking a familiar pose, ball under his right arm, left arm jutting out to straight-arm a would-be tackler. A few days later, Howard won the Heisman.

When he blossomed as a Packer after four undistinguished seasons in the NFL, Howard apparently decided that trash-talking and high-stepping might make people more aware of his gifts. He repeated the Heisman pose only once, after a 92-yard punt return against the Lions in Detroit, appropriately close to his alma mater in Ann Arbor. But after that, Desmond, a confessed cartoon addict, chose to model some of his steps on the moves of cartoon characters. He was certainly a roadrunner, and no one would deny that he was animated.

After Desmond's dash, the Patriots started on their own 25-yard line. Bledsoe passed to Byars for 5 yards. *Perhaps they could come back once more.*

Reggie White personally wiped out such thoughts.

On second and five, Bledsoe dropped back to pass again. Lined up at left end, opposite New England tackle Max Lane, White made a move to the outside. Lane, trying to stay in front of him, shuffled sideways, and as he did, White swung his right arm, his familiar ``club'' move, a potent weapon for more than a decade, and the blow knocked the 305-pound Lane off his feet. White drove inside and pounced on Bledsoe, buried the quarterback for an 8-yard loss.

On third and 13, Bledsoe again dropped back, and Lane again faced White, wary now of Reggie's club. Lane cheated toward the inside, and Reggie, in command now, sprang to the outside, protected himself with a raised right arm. It was Bledsoe who needed the protection. White dropped him again, for a 6-yard loss. Two straight sacks—after two straight playoff games without a single sack.

New England, thoroughly defused, never threatened to score in the final eighteen minutes, never even got close to midfield. The Patriots produced only one first down the whole quarter, and on the next play, Craig Newsome picked off Bledsoe, the third of Green Bay's four interceptions.

In each of the Packers' three playoff games, in front of live audiences of almost 200,000 people and television audiences of almost a billion, Craig Newsome came up with an interception, an unprecedented streak, an NFL playoff record. The crowd, the pressure, the spotlight, nothing fazed Newsome. But all season long Newsome did not sit for a single live television interview. He was too frightened.

Obviously, Newsome is two different people, quiet and shy off the field, cocky and vicious on the field, almost incapable of holding back, even in practice. Opposing quarterbacks sometimes suspect that he is two different people *on* the field, maybe three.

Like Don Beebe, Newsome did not feel he was ready for college straight out of high school. He spent two years as a block mason. He built brick walls. Now he ___ ___ ___. It does not require a degree in English to complete the previous sentence.

The entire defensive backfield—Newsome and Evans at the corners, Butler and Robinson at the safeties, a matched quartet, all within half an inch of six feet tall, all within 10 pounds of weighing 200—started every game in 1996 and every game in 1995, which helps to explain their cohesiveness. The only difference was that in 1995, Robinson was starting for Seattle, not Green Bay. His presence in Green Bay also helps to explain the foursome's cohesiveness.

Robinson is the elder statesman, the wise veteran; he has spent twelve seasons in the NFL, only one less than Butler, Evans, and Newsome combined. The three youngsters were all draft choices, Newsome a first-rounder, Butler a second. Robinson was a free agent, lightly regarded when he entered Colgate University, a 150- or 155-pound walk-on, not much heavier or more heavily regarded when he graduated. He entered the NFL as a free agent, scrapping for a job, and he still plays, he says, with a free-agent mentality, his admirable work ethic inspired by the awareness that he could lose his job any minute.

Robinson majored in computer science in college and plays the saxophone for enjoyment, and he blends science and rhythm on the football field, too. His ability to figure out tendencies, to anticipate plays and moves, enables his backfield mates to play more aggressively, to blitz and gamble on interceptions. He led the backfield with six interceptions in 1996, second in the NFL—he leads all active NFL players with forty-eight career interceptions—but Evans and Butler were right behind him, with five apiece. As a team, the Packers picked off twenty-six passes in 1996, twice as many as they intercepted in 1995. Maturity was the difference, Robinson's and his teammates'. Each of the foursome turned in more than seventy tackles, roughly five apiece per game. Butler led with eighty-eight, and with six-and-a-half sacks, the most ever for a defensive back.

If Robinson does not hold the world record for autographs and interviews, he is, at worst, a contender. He loves his teammates, talks about not wanting to let them down, and he loves Green Bay, and talks about not letting the people down. His home in Green Bay is a magnet for kids in the 'hood, an open house. "As great an athlete as he is," his coach, Mike Holmgren says, "he's even a greater person." Robinson calls Holmgren "Coach Dad," and says, "He doesn't want anything to go wrong."

When Robinson arrived in Green Bay, one of the first people he met told him, "It would behoove you to learn Packer history." Robinson behooved himself,

now tosses names like Thurston and Wood and Adderley into casual conversation. "This town is unique,"
he says. "People send me thank-you letters, thanking
me for becoming a Packer."

It was inevitable that Robinson would become a
Packer. In Hartford, Connecticut, his high school
team's colors were green and gold.

Ron Wolf is probably not a genius, not in the class
of a Mozart or an Einstein, a Shakespeare or a Michel-
angelo. But when it comes to judging football talent
and character, he is a da Vinci or, at least, an Al Davis.
In 1996, Wolf acquired Desmond Howard, Santana
Dotson, Ron Cox, and Don Beebe as free agents and
traded for Eugene Robinson. Three Super Bowl starters
and one Super Bowl superstar. Good people, too, solid
citizens. Which wasn't an accident.

"You cannot separate the football player from what
he does off the field," Eugene Robinson says.

"I don't have to worry about these guys when they
leave the game," his coach, Fritz Shurmur, says.

Bob Harlan, the Packers' president, points out that
the character of a player is magnified in a community
as small as Green Bay, that his indiscretions are much
more visible.

The Packers understand this. The vast majority of
them are not the kind of people who do not care what
other people think of them.

Reggie White, Keith Jackson, Eugene Robinson and
Don Beebe are serious Christians, but they are not sanc-
timonious. White and Robinson, particularly, recall

the wilderness periods in their past, the days when they sinned. They do not scorn or scold teammates. They set examples.

Mike Holmgren took the individuals Wolf gave him and molded them into a team, no easy feat in an age of enormous salaries and matching egos. They all came to Green Bay proud of themselves. Holmgren made them proud of each other, proud of the organization, proud of the town. It's a chicken-and-egg proposition whether success produces team spirit, or vice versa—I lean toward the former—but Green Bay enjoyed both in abundance.

Holmgren seldom raged, but he was always firm. Once, Reggie White and Sean Jones came to him and suggested that he was intimidating the young players. They offered to help out, to discipline and motivate the young players themselves, to free Holmgren for what they considered more important things. "I appreciate your having this talk with me," Holmgren said, "but I can't do that."

Holmgren recalls the meeting with amusement. "Reggie is a wonderful person and an awesome player," the coach says, "but in his own way he's very naïve. Sean is very bright, but he's a con man. I know that he's full of shit, and he knows that I know. We get along perfectly."

Jones and Holmgren did not get along perfectly at one point during the playoff game against San Francisco. Jones was beaten on one play, and George Koonce yelled something at him, and when Jones spun and shoved Koonce, Holmgren turned to Gabe Wilkins, a backup defensive end, and said, "Get in the game, and get his ass out of there!"

Fritz Shurmur started to argue, trying to defend his defenders, seeking to keep the starting defense intact. "Oh, geez," Shurmur began, and Holmgren said, "No, you don't do that, that's not right." Wilkins went in, and Jones came to the sidelines and tried to talk to Holmgren. "I don't want to talk to you," Holmgren said. "Sit your ass down." And Jones did.

"I have to do that," Holmgren says. "And I have to be me. They know I don't rant and rave all the time, so when I do . . ."

Holmgren believes in being firm. He also believes in being fair. But most of all he believes in being knowledgeable. "I think knowing the game, knowing what you're doing," he says, "is the most important part of coaching. If you can't make your players believe you know what you're doing, you can't get them to do anything."

The Super Bowl, Don Beebe says, was "the greatest-called game I have ever been a part of." Beebe has total respect for his Buffalo coach, Marv Levy, but, he says, "Coach Holmgren implemented the perfect scheme for this game."

On the Patriots' final possession, on first and ten, Reggie White swung his club once more, and once more leveled Max Lane and Drew Bledsoe, his third sack, a Super Bowl record.

"That's the big dog," Gilbert Brown said. *"He's amazing."*

Willie Davis applauded the big dog. "Up till the sacks, he'd played a game that wouldn't have distinguished him from other linemen," Davis said. "They'd been doubling him a lot. Then he stepped up."

"I couldn't believe they didn't double-team him there," Dave Robinson said. "I thought for sure after the first sack, absolutely for sure after the second sack. I can't understand the thinking there."

"They held Reggie all year," said Lionel Aldridge, who watched the game on television in Milwaukee. "Finally, in this game, he got up against a guy who didn't hold him."

Aldridge, like Reggie and like Willie Davis, was a defensive end. "I don't think there's anybody in football that compares to Reggie White," he said.

Reggie White finished the first Super Bowl of his glittering career with the most devastating statistics a quarterback could imagine: Three sacks, seven hurries, seven hits.

The final score was devastating, too: Green Bay 35, New England 21—a push for the bookmakers who had decided the Packers were a fourteen-point favorite, a thirteenth straight defeat for the American Football Conference.

Jerry Kramer was never much of a fan of sacks—he had always preferred to see quarterbacks upright—but Reggie White's three sacks were his favorite part of Super Bowl XXXI. "I knew it was going to be a great thrill for Reggie just to be in the ball game," Kramer says, "but it was a great kick for me to see those three almost in a row. I just said, 'Super! What a great deal! Good for him!' I knew the old man was wanting it, and I felt real good about that."

Kramer probably did not stop to calculate that "old man" White was younger than Jerry's oldest son.

Reggie White, legitimately, could have been named the Most Valuable Player in Super Bowl XXXI. His numbers plus his leadership would have justified the choice.

Brett Favre, legitimately, could have been named the Most Valuable Player in Super Bowl XXXI. He had completed fourteen of twenty-seven passes for 246 yards and two touchdowns without an interception. He had also run for a touchdown. Quarterbacks had been named the MVP of a Super Bowl with less gaudy numbers.

At the end of Super Bowl II, when Bart Starr, who had completed thirteen of twenty-four passes for 202 yards and one touchdown without an interception, was named the Most Valuable Player for the second year in a row, Pat Chandler demanded a recount. After all, her husband, Don Chandler, had outscored Oakland all by himself. Chandler had four field goals, three extra points, a total of fifteen points. The Raiders had a total of fourteen.

In Super Bowl XXXI, the Most Valuable Player award went to neither a defensive player nor an offensive player, but to the star of the Packers' special teams, Desmond Howard, a handsome little complement to his Heisman Trophy.

Howard, the $300,000 bargain, returned six punts for 90 yards and four kickoffs for 154 yards. His first punt return set up the game's first touchdown, another set up a field goal, and his record-breaking kickoff return provided the game's decisive touchdown.

His sudden bursts of speed were as dazzling as his smile, as devastating as the trash talk he fired back at hecklers on the New England sidelines. "If you're going to start jawing with me," Howard said after the game, "I'm not going to sit back and take it. I know how to curse, too."

When the Super Bowl ended, Jerry Kramer felt a tremendous sense of relief. "No jealousy," he says. "No pain. No fear that they're not gonna love us anymore. I felt like I had become a part of the new team."

"I felt a kinship really," Lionel Aldridge said. "It made me very proud."

"I love the Green Bay Packers," Marv Fleming said.

"I'm so happy for the players and the town," Bart Starr said.

In Florida, Paul Hornung raised his glass of water and toasted the Packers. Hornung said he had won his Super Bowl bet. "I got down early," he explained. "I was only giving twelve and a half."

Of course. Hornung never met a bet he didn't win.

*   *   *

Kramer sat in the stands and watched the presentation of the Lombardi Trophy to the new Green Bay Packers. "I didn't want to leave the Superdome," he said. Twenty-nine years earlier, in Miami, after Super Bowl II, after the last game he played for Vince Lombardi, Kramer didn't want to leave the Orange Bowl.

"I sat in front of my locker, and I talked and talked and talked," Kramer wrote in *Instant Replay*. "I talked about the spirit of our team. I talked about Lombardi. I really didn't want to get up. I wanted to keep my uniform on as long as I possibly could."

Kramer looked at the celebrating Packers in the Superdome and said, out loud, "Now it's your turn."

For winning Super Bowl XXXI, the Packers earned $48,000 apiece, $33,000 a man more than the Super Bowl I Packers. For some of them, like quarterback Kyle Wachholtz and guard Marco Rivera, a pair of rookies who were late-round draft choices and didn't appear in a game all season, $48,000 was a munificent bonus. For Reggie White and Brett Favre, with their multi-million-dollar salaries, $48,000 was a sizable cut in pay. None of the four complained.

"I want to be remembered as the best to ever play the game," Brett Favre said. "There are only a few things that are important to me, and that's one of them."

Favre also wants to be the best-paid ever to play the game. That's one of the few things that is important to his agent.

*   *   *

Mike Holmgren held the Lombardi Trophy firmly in his hand. "You see this," he said. "You see whose name is on it? This means a lot to any player, but it means more to us. This trophy belongs in Green Bay."

Ron Pitts, getting ready to conduct locker-room interviews for Fox's postgame show, choked up on Holmgren's words. "I swear I almost cried," Pitts said. "I just started thinking about all the pictures of Vince and my father around our house and all the rings he has. That was a hell of a moment."

Holmgren looked around the locker room. "I'm so proud of you," he continued. "We set our goals in July, and you made every single goal. You earned it. You worked for it. And before we came out for the second half, what did you do? You locked arms. Do it right now, men. To the coaches, players, trainers, the equipment people, everybody, this trophy is for you, men. Everybody. Everyone had a say in it. Everyone got it done. I'm proud of you."

And once again Keith Jackson triggered the familiar chant:

"Who we?"

"Packers!"

"Who we?"

"Packers!"

"Who we?"

"Packers! Whoooooo!"

*   *   *

Strangely, the Packers' locker room after the Super Bowl was relatively subdued, not nearly so jubilant as after the Carolina game. There were a variety of reasons, including the presence of outsiders, Fox television crews and reporters, members of the Board of Directors, NFL officials, and the absence of key players, spirited away to press conferences and to live television interviews on the field. Perhaps, too, there was a feeling of relief, a sense of avoiding failure, of not letting down the city or the fans, the coaches or themselves. Dorsey Levens sobbed openly. Reggie White and Andre Rison and Antonio Freeman cried, too, tears of joy and relief.

Adam Timmerman had a big smile on his face. "Fuzzy told me I had to get one of those rings of my own," he said. "When I get it, I'll have to bring it by and show it to him."

"It's been a real long week," Frank Winters said. "I wish my brother could have been here."

Don Beebe stood in the interview area, clutching the Lombardi Trophy, and thought of his Buffalo teammates. "I just wish those guys could feel what I feel right now," he said. Beebe also thought of his Green Bay teammates. He said they didn't know it yet, but he was going to take the Lombardi Trophy home and display it in his foyer. "I've been wanting to hold this thing for a long time," he said.

*   *   *

Edgar Bennett said he couldn't believe the Packers had won the Super Bowl. He said it was an "unbelievable feeling." He also said it was "an unbelievable moment." He added, "I completely can't believe this experience." Nobody believed him.

Bennett hugged LeRoy Butler and told him, "We finally got us a championship. After high school, college, we finally got ourselves a championship. Never had one. We have the greatest one now."

Bennett also talked of his feelings for his fellow Packers. "I love my teammates," he said. "I really do. They're so down to earth. From Brett and Reggie down. No one's out to get anybody. No one's out to embarrass anybody."

Antonio Freeman seconded Bennett's opinion. "Everybody's down to earth," he said, surrounded by teammates who were sky high.

"When you win the big one in high school," Aaron Taylor said, "there is always something bigger. When you win the big one in college, there is always something bigger. But when you win this one—this is as big as it gets!"

Santana Dotson came up with a terrific idea. He said the trip would have been more fun if the Packers had played the game first, the day they arrived, and then celebrated Super Bowl Week in New Orleans.

*   *   *

"I think we are America's team," Brett Favre said. "I do. If you rode around the city today, like we did on the way to the stadium, it was unbelievable. It was like a home game."

When he was asked what made the Packers America's team, Favre said, "I just think it's a down-home personality. We're owned not by one person, but by a bunch of people, by the city, basically. We win with class and we lose with class. We have fun and people like to watch us play. It's Green Bay. It's small-town America."

The man on the phone was, like Barry Switzer and Jerry Jones, born in a small town in Arkansas. He said he'd like to speak to Mike Holmgren. "It's the White House," the coach was informed. He took the call.

"Congratulations," President Clinton said. "I had a feeling you were going to have a good year when I visited you at the start of the season."

"Well, we've both had pretty good years," Holmgren said.

Holmgren is not especially superstitious, but he knows enough not to change a winning pattern. "I'd like to invite you to come back out next fall," he told the President.

The President clearly was pleased for the Packers even if they didn't have a single player from the University of Arkansas or from any of his alma maters, Georgetown, Yale or Oxford. Mr. Clinton did, however, have geographical ties to two Packers: Keith Jackson, who was born and raised in Arkansas, and Desmond Howard, who arrived in Washington in 1992 and was criticized for not delivering all he promised.

The President spoke to Desmond, too, and congratulated him on the Most Valuable Player award. Mr. Clinton was happy to know there is life after Washington.

The President did not speak to Reggie White. The Minister of Defense was not happy with the Commander-in-Chief. When Mr. Clinton visited Lambeau Field before the season, he told Reggie he would try to help him rebuild his church. Reggie never heard again from the White House. Maybe he shouldn't have supported the Republican in the race for sheriff.

On the last of the Packer buses heading back to the Fairmont, LeRoy Butler reflected on the season and decided that the main reason for the team's success was its selflessness, its lack of ego. Andre Rison said he couldn't agree more. Andre also said he was glad that he had gotten a chance to show that he was the greatest receiver in the whole world.

Rison actually is quite charming. He is totally lacking in guile, if not in self-confidence.

In the confused rush to escape from the Superdome, to start the celebration, the Packers' medical staff forgot Antonio Freeman, or at least forgot the cast on his left forearm. Without a doctor in sight, Freeman had to go to the team's equipment managers, who tracked down a buzzsaw in the Superdome and carved off the cast without amputating Antonio's arm.

At the victory party, in the Fairmont Hotel, the air was of satisfaction more than exhilaration. On Bourbon Street and its tributaries, of course, Packer fans, young and old, male and female, black and white, from Wisconsin and West Virginia, went absolutely crazy.

They deserved it.

The following morning, Peggy Kostelnik Spaulding, who had watched the Super Bowl with a mixture of joy and sadness, found herself on an elevator at the Fairmont with Antonio Freeman. She smiled at him and said, "Treasure this moment."

"Her husband played on the first Super Bowl team," another passenger explained to Freeman.

"We value everything that team taught us," Freeman said. "They taught us how to do it."

It was Freeman's turn to smile. "And we really appreciate your support," he said.

The Green Bay Packers received a million and a half phone calls inquiring into the Super Bowl celebration that was held the day after the game at Lambeau Field. The tickets for the welcome-home party sold out in four hours, and when the buses carrying the Packers from Austin Straubel Airport to the stadium were delayed by traffic and delirium, many of the ticketholders sat in the stands far longer than that, shivering with cold and anticipation.

*   *   *

The National Football League reported that sales of Super Bowl XXXI merchandise soared to a record $130 million. Fans and frontrunners bought 650,000 Packer locker-room hats, hats displayed for the first time right after the game; the previous record for championship headwear was 400,000, set by the NBA's Chicago Bulls the previous spring. More than 125,000 copies of the Packers' highlight video were sold within two weeks after they went on sale.

The Packers were a green-and-gold mine. The team itself reported record profits of more than $5.5 million for the Super Bowl season. The value of the team headed toward $200 million.

In the week after the Super Bowl, Jerry Kramer noticed that his phone had stopped ringing. He kind of liked the sound. "It's like closure," he said.

Vince Lombardi Jr. shared Kramer's feeling. "I'm just so happy," he said, "that the people in Green Bay can now live in today rather than yesterday."

The ghosts had been exorcised.

Epilogue

In 2027, thirty years after Super Bowl XXXI, will the Packers of the nineties still be embraced by the city of Green Bay, and by each other, the way the Packers of the sixties were still embraced in 1997, thirty years after Super Bowl I?

I doubt it.

The world of sports has changed so much.

In the sixties, when athletes had far less money and lots more fun, when free agency was only a dream and no one wore salary caps, winning teams stayed together. Seventeen of the men who put on Packer uniforms for Super Bowl I or Super Bowl II spent nine or more seasons in Green Bay.

Herb Adderley, Lionel Aldridge, Ken Bowman, Willie Davis, Boyd Dowler, Forrest Gregg, Paul Hornung, Jerry Kramer, Max McGee, Ray Nitschke, Elijah Pitts, Dave

Robinson, Bob Skoronski, Bart Starr, Jim Taylor, Fuzzy Thurston, and Willie Woods—all of them Packers for periods ranging from nine years to sixteen. Three of them—Davis, Dowler, and Gregg—never missed a game in their lengthy careers in green and gold.

The people of Green Bay knew their names as well as they knew the names of their neighbors or their children. Even today, almost everyone over forty, male or female, college graduate or high-school dropout, can recite both starting lineups, offense and defense. The names trip from the tongue eagerly, smoothly, a litany of legends.

Those of us ancient enough to have been Brooklyn Dodger fans in the late forties and early fifties can do the same thing: Campanella catching, Hodges at first, Robinson at second, Reese at short, Cox at third, Snider in center, Furillo in right, Newcombe and Roe and Erskine and Black on the mound. A little trouble with left field: Pafko, Shuba, Abrams, Amoros and others took turns out there. Pafko was the best of the lot, Amoros the most memorable.

But not one of the Super Bowl XXXI Packers had spent nine seasons in Green Bay, and most of them never would. LeRoy Butler and Brett Favre, they'd probably make it. Mark Chmura and Edgar Bennett and Robert Brooks, they might. All the rest are long shots.

Less than six weeks after Super Bowl XXXI, the team began to change. Desmond Howard, the MVP of the Super Bowl, the hero of so many victories in his one Packer season, accepted the Oakland Raiders' offer of

$6 million for four seasons, a million and a half a year, five times what he made in Green Bay. No one could seriously fault him. The Packers couldn't afford to keep him; he couldn't afford to stay. He didn't just take the money and run. He ran and took the money.

Gilbert Brown, who is twice Desmond's size, could have gotten twice Desmond's money. The Jacksonville Jaguars were offering him $3 million a year. But Brown, who played for only $275,000 in 1996, elected to stay with the Packers, partly, he says, because, after he signed an autograph for a young girl, she looked at him and said, "Don't leave," and he saw tears in her eyes. He was touched. He was touched, too, when Green Bay gave him $8.25 million for three years, an average of $2,750,000 a season, only a few pennies below the Jacksonville bid.

In the weeks that followed, Jim McMahon and Keith Jackson both decided to retire, McMahon heading toward the golf course, Jackson toward the broadcast booth. The Packers elected not to offer contracts to Andre Rison, who was expensive and, with Brooks recuperating smartly, expendable; or to Sean Jones, who was aging. Ron Wolf drafted a placekicker in the third round, a signal that Chris Jacke's Green Bay tour, the longest of any member of the 1996 team, was over.

In a rare public-relations debacle, the Packers did not invite Jacke, Rison, or Howard to go with their 1996 teammates to the White House, to be hailed by the Chief. All three were hurt, and fans were annoyed unnecessarily.

Other players will leave before the 1997 season

opens, but Favre and Freeman, Butler and Brooks, White and Newsome, Bennett and Beebe, Chmura and Winters, Evans and the Dotsons—the nucleus and more—will be back. Green Bay fans will recognize most of the names, most of the faces in 1997 and 1998. After that, not even Ron Wolf knows.

"We want to win back-to-back," Mark Chmura says.

Their coach, whose base salary will leap to more than a million dollars in 1997, decided long before training camp began to give up the subsidiary income of his television and radio shows. He intends to devote part of the time he will save to his family—his youngest daughter, Gretchen, has only two more years at home—and part of it to doing everything possible to win again. "I wanted to set an example for the players," Holmgren says. "It's hard to repeat."

But it's possible, especially if Favre and most of his teammates stay healthy. They are the preseason favorites.

Only six teams have won back-to-back Super Bowls. Dallas. San Francisco. Miami. Pittsburgh twice.

And, of course, the first team to do it, the Green Bay Packers of Super Bowl I and Super Bowl II.

You can't forget them.

ROSTERS AND STATISTICS

No.	Name	Pos.	Ht.	Wt.	Age	College	Hometown
82	Don Beebe	WR	5–11	183	32	Chadron State	Aurora, Ill.
34	Edgar Bennett	RB	6–0	217	27	Florida State	Jacksonville, Fla.
87	*Robert Brooks	WR	6–0	180	26	South Carolina	Greenwood, S.C.
68	Gary Brown	T/G	6–4	315	25	Georgia Tech	Amityville, N.Y.
93	Gilbert Brown	DT	6–2	325	25	Kansas	Farmington, Mich.
36	LeRoy Butler	S	6–0	200	28	Florida State	Jacksonville, Fla.
89	Mark Chmura	TE	6–5	250	27	Boston College	Deerfield, Mass.
91	Shannon Clavelle	DE	6–2	287	23	Colorado	Lafayette, La.
54	Ron Cox	LB	6–2	235	28	Fresno State	Fresno, Calif.
67	Jeff Dellenbach	C	6–6	300	33	Wisconsin	Wausau, Wis.
72	Earl Dotson	T	6–3½	315	26	Texas A&I	Beaumont, Tex.
71	Santana Dotson	DT	6–5	285	27	Baylor	New Orleans, La.
33	Doug Evans	CB	6–0½	190	26	Louisiana Tech	Shreveport, La.
4	Brett Favre	QB	6–2	225	27	Southern Mississippi	Gulfport, Miss.
86	Antonio Freeman	WR	6–0½	190	24	Virginia Tech	Baltimore, Md.
55	Bernardo Harris	LB	6–2	243	25	North Carolina	Chapel Hill, N.C.

254

No.	Name	Pos.	Ht.	Wt.	Age	College	Hometown
40	Chris Hayes	S	6-0	200	24	Washington State	San Bernardino, Calif.
30	William Henderson	FB	6-1½	248	25	North Carolina	Richmond, Va.
17	Craig Hentrich	P	6-3	200	25	Notre Dame	Alton, Ill.
90	Darius Holland	DT	6-4½	310	23	Colorado	Petersburg, Va.
56	Lamont Hollinquest	LB	6-3	243	26	Southern California	Los Angeles, Calif.
81	Desmond Howard	WR	5-10	180	26	Michigan	Cleveland, Ohio
13	Chris Jacke	PK	6-0	205	30	Texas-El Paso	Richmond, Va.
88	Keith Jackson	TE	6-2	258	31	Oklahoma	Little Rock, Ark.
32	Travis Jervey	RB	5-11½	225	25	The Citadel	Columbia, S.C.
27	Calvin Jones	RB	5-11	205	26	Nebraska	Omaha, Neb.
96	Sean Jones	DE	6-7	283	34	Northeastern	Kingston, Jamaica
65	Lindsay Knapp	G	6-6	300	26	Notre Dame	Arlington Heights, Ill.
53	#George Koonce	LB	6-1	243	28	East Carolina	New Bern, N.C.
94	Bob Kuberski	DT	6-4½	295	25	Navy	Chester, Pa.
25	Dorsey Levens	RB	6-1	235	26	Georgia Tech	Syracuse, N.Y.
80	Derrick Mayes	WR	6-0½	200	22	Notre Dame	Indianapolis, Ind.

No.	Name	Pos.	Ht.	Wt.	Age	College	Hometown
95	Keith McKenzie	DE/LB	6–2½	242	23	Ball State	Highland Park, Mich.
9	Jim McMahon	QB	6–1	195	37	Brigham Young	Jersey City, N.J.
77	John Michels	T	6–7	290	23	Southern California	La Jolla, Calif.
85	Terry Mickens	WR	6–0½	198	25	Florida A&M	Tallahassee, Fla.
28	Roderick Mullen	CB/S	6–1	204	24	Grambling State	St. Francisville, La.
21	Craig Newsome	CB	5–11½	190	25	Arizona State	San Bernardino, Calif.
18	Doug Pederson	QB	6–3	215	28	Northeast Louisiana	Bellingham, Wash.
39	Mike Prior	S	6–0	208	33	Illinois State	Chicago Heights, Ill.
84	Andre Rison	WR	6–1	195	29	Michigan State	Flint, Mich.
62	Marco Rivera	G	6–4	295	24	Penn State	Elmont, N.Y.
41	Eugene Robinson	S	6–0	195	33	Colgate	Hartford, Conn.
46	Michael Robinson	CB	6–1	192	23	Hampton	King & Queen, Va.
75	‡Ken Ruettgers	T	6–6	295	34	Southern California	Bakersfield, Calif.
59	Wayne Simmons	LB	6–2½	248	27	Clemson	Beaufort, S.C.
73	Aaron Taylor	G	6–4	305	24	Notre Dame	San Francisco, Calif.

No.	Name	Pos.	Ht.	Wt.	Age	College	Hometown
83	Jeff Thomason	TE	6–4½	250	27	Oregon	San Diego, Calif.
63	Adam Timmerman	G	6–4	295	25	South Dakota State	Cherokee, Iowa
7	Kyle Wachholtz	QB	6–4	235	24	Southern California	Fullerton, Calif.
92	Reggie White	DE	6–5	300	35	Tennessee	Chattanooga, Tenn.
64	Bruce Wilkerson	T	6–5	305	32	Tennessee	Loudon, Tenn.
98	Gabe Wilkins	DE	6–4½	305	25	Gardner-Webb	Spartanburg, S.C.
51	Brian Williams	LB	6–1½	235	24	Southern California	Dallas, Tex.
37	Tyrone Williams	CB	5–11	195	23	Nebraska	Bradenton, Fla.
52	Frank Winters	C	6–3	295	32	Western Illinois	Hoboken, N.J.

*Injured Week Seven vs. San Francisco (out for season)

#Injured in Divisional Playoffs vs. San Francisco (out for season)

‡Retired following Week Eleven at Dallas

REGULAR SEASON

Date			GB	Opp.	Attend.
Sept. 1	at Tampa Bay Buccaneers	W	34	3	54,102
Sept. 9	Philadelphia Eagles	W	39	13	60,666
Sept. 15	San Diego Chargers	W	42	10	60,584
Sept. 22	at Minnesota Vikings	L	21	30	64,168
Sept. 29	at Seattle Seahawks	W	31	10	59,973
Oct. 6	at Chicago Bears	W	37	6	65,480
Oct. 14	San Francisco 49ers (OT)	W	23	20	60,716
Oct. 27	Tampa Bay Buccaneers	W	13	7	60,627
Nov. 3	Detroit Lions	W	28	18	60,695
Nov. 10	at Kansas City Chiefs	L	20	27	79,281
Nov. 18	at Dallas Cowboys	L	6	21	65,032
Nov. 24	at St. Louis Rams	W	24	9	61,499
Dec. 1	Chicago Bears	W	28	17	59,682
Dec. 8	Denver Broncos	W	41	6	60,712
Dec. 15	at Detroit Lions	W	31	3	73,214
Dec. 22	Minnesota Vikings	W	38	10	59,306

POSTSEASON

Date			GB	Opp.	Attend.
Jan. 4	San Francisco 49ers	W	35	14	60,787
Jan. 12	Carolina Panthers	W	30	13	60,216
Jan. 26	New England Patriots	W	35	21	72,301

SCORING	TD	Ru	Pa	Rt	K-PAT	FG	S	PTS
Jacke	0	0	0	0	51/53	21/27	0	114
Jackson	10	0	10	0			0	60
Levens	10	5	5	0			0	60
Freeman	9	0	9	0			0	54
Beebe	6	0	4	2			0	36
R. Brooks	4	0	4	0			0	24
Bennett	3	2	1	0			0	22
Howard	3	0	0	3			0	18
Rison-Jax./G.B.	3	0	3	0			0	18
Rison-G.B.	1	0	1	0			0	6
Favre	2	2	0	0			0	12
Mayes	2	0	2	0			0	12
Mickens	2	0	2	0			0	12
Butler	1	0	0	1			0	6
Evans	1	0	0	1			0	6
Henderson	1	0	1	0			0	6
Koonce	1	0	0	1			0	6
TEAM	56	9	39	8	51/53	21/27	1	456
OPPONENTS	19	7	12	0	17/17	25/27	1	210

2-Pt. Conversions: Bennett 2, TEAM 2–3, OPPONENTS 1–2

PASSING	Att.	Cmp.	Yds.	Cmp%	TD	Int.	Long	Rating
Favre	543	325	3899	59.9	39	13	80t	95.8
McMahon	4	3	39	75.0	0	0	24	105.2
Hentrich	1	0	0	0	0	0	0	39.6
TEAM	548	328	3938	59.9	39	13	80t	95.7
OPPONENTS	544	283	2942	52.0	12	26	69	55.4

RUSHING	No.	Yds.	Avg.	Long	TD
Bennett	222	899	4.0	23	2
Levens	121	566	4.7	24	5
Favre	49	136	2.8	23	2
Henderson	39	130	3.3	14	0
Jervey	26	106	4.1	12	0
R. Brooks	4	2	0.5	6	0
McMahon	4	−1	−0.3	2	0
TEAM	465	1838	4.0	24	9
OPPONENTS	400	1416	3.5	37t	7

RECEIVING	No.	Yds.	Avg.	Long	TD
Freeman	56	933	16.7	51t	9
Rison-Jax./G.B.	47	593	12.6	61t	3
Rison-G.B.	13	135	10.4	22t	1
Jackson	40	505	12.6	51t	10
Beebe	39	699	17.9	80t	4
Levens	31	226	7.3	49	5
Bennett	31	176	5.7	25t	1
Chmura	28	370	13.2	29	0
Henderson	27	203	7.5	27	0
R. Brooks	23	344	15.0	38	4
Mickens	18	161	8.9	19	2
Howard	13	95	7.3	12	0
Mayes	6	46	7.7	12	2
Thomason	3	45	15.0	24	0
TEAM	328	3938	12.0	80t	39
OPPONENTS	283	2942	10.4	69	12

INTERCEPTIONS	No.	Yds.	Avg.	Long	TD
E. Robinson	6	107	17.8	39	0
Butler	5	149	29.8	90t	1
Evans	5	102	20.4	63	1
Koonce	3	84	28.0	75t	1
Newsome	2	22	11.0	20	0
White	1	46	46.0	46	0
Prior	1	7	7.0	7	0
Dowden	1	5	5.0	5	0
Hollinquest	1	2	2.0	2	0
Simmons	1	0	0.0	0	0
TEAM	26	524	20.2	90t	3
OPPONENTS	13	98	7.5	41	0

PUNTING	No.	Yds.	Avg.	Net	TB	In20	LG	Blk.
Hentrich	68	2886	42.4	36.3	9	28	65	0
TEAM	68	2886	42.4	36.3	9	28	65	0
OPPONENTS	90	3876	43.1	32.5	4	15	63	1

PUNT RETURNS	Ret.	FC	Yds.	Avg.	Long	TD
Howard	58	16	875	15.1	92t	3
Prior	0	1	0	0.0	0	0
TEAM	58	17	875	15.1	92t	3
OPPONENTS	29	15	237	8.2	26	0

KICKOFF RETURNS	No.	Yds.	Avg.	Long	TD
Howard	22	460	20.9	40	0
Beebe	15	403	26.9	90t	1
Levens	5	84	16.8	29	0
Henderson	2	38	19.0	23	0
Thomason	1	20	20.0	20	0
Jervey	1	17	17.0	17	0
Freeman	1	16	16.0	16	0
TEAM	47	1038	22.1	90t	1
OPPONENTS	76	1649	21.7	45	0

FIELD GOALS	1–19	20–29	30–39	40–49	50+
Jacke	0/0	6/6	9/11	5/9	1/1
TEAM	0/0	6/6	9/11	5/9	1/1
OPPONENTS	0/0	4/5	9/9	12/13	0/0

SUNDAY, JANUARY 12, 1997

Carolina	7	3	3	0—13
Green Bay	0	17	10	3—30

SCORING

FIRST QUARTER

CP   H. Griffith 3 yd. pass from K. Collins (J. Kasay, kick)

SECOND QUARTER

GB   D. Levens 29 yd. pass from B. Favre (C. Jacke, kick)

CP   J. Kasay 22 yd. Field Goal

GB   A. Freeman 6 yd. pass from B. Favre (C. Jacke, kick)

GB   C. Jacke 31 yd. Field Goal

THIRD QUARTER

GB   C. Jacke 32 yd. Field Goal

CP   J. Kasay 23 yd. Field Goal

GB   E. Bennett 4 yd. run (C. Jacke, kick)

FOURTH QUARTER

GB   C. Jacke 28 yd. Field Goal

TEAM STATISTICS

	Packers	Panthers
First Downs	22	12
Total Net Yards	479	251
Total Plays	75	53
Net Yards Rushing	201	45
Net Yards Passing	278	206
Passes (A-C-I)	29–19–1	37–19–2
Penalties-Yards	5–45	4–25
Fumbles (No.-Lost)	2–1	2–1

RUSHING

Packers: Bennett 25–99; Levens 10–88; Favre 5–14; McMahon 4–0; Henderson 1–0.

Panthers: Johnson 11–31; Oliver 2–15; Collins 1–(–1).

RECEIVING

Packers: Levens 5–117; Freeman 4–43; Rison 3–53; Jackson 3–30; Bennett 2–5; Beebe 1–29; Chmura 1–15.

Panthers: Green 5–51; Carrier 4–65; Griffith 4–23; Walls 3–33; Ismail 1–24; Johnson 1–14; Oliver 1–5.

PASSING

Packers: Favre 29–19–1 (292 yards).

Panthers: Collins 37–19–2 (215 yards).

266

SUNDAY, JANUARY 26, 1997

New England	14	0	7	0—21
Green Bay	10	17	8	0—35

SCORING

FIRST QUARTER

GB   A. Rison 54 yd. pass from B. Favre (C. Jacke, kick)

GB   C. Jacke 37 yd. Field Goal

NE   K. Byars 1 yd. pass from D. Bledsoe (A. Vinatieri, kick)

NE   B. Coates 4 yd. pass from D. Bledsoe (A. Vinatieri, kick)

SECOND QUARTER

GB   A. Freeman 81 yd. pass from B. Favre (C. Jacke, kick)

GB   C. Jacke 31 yd. Field Goal

GB   B. Favre 2 yd. run (C. Jacke, kick)

THIRD QUARTER

NE   C. Martin 18 yd. run (A. Vinatieri, kick)

GB   D. Howard 99 yd. kickoff return (M. Chmura-B. Favre, pass)

TEAM STATISTICS

	Packers	Patriots
First Downs	16	16
Total Net Yards	323	257
Total Plays	68	66
Net Yards Rushing	115	43
Net Yards Passing	208	214
Passes (A-C-I)	27–14–0	48–25–4
Penalties-Yards	3–41	2–22
Fumbles (No.-Lost)	0–0	0–0

RUSHING

Packers: Bennett 17–40; Levens 14–61; Favre 4–12; Henderson 1–2.

Patriots: Martin 11–42; Bledsoe 1–1; Meggett 1–0.

RECEIVING

Packers: Freeman 3–105; Levens 3–23; Rison 2–77; Henderson 2–14; Chmura 2–13; Jackson 1–10; Bennett 1–4.

Patriots: Coates 6–67; Glenn 4–62; Byars 4–42; Jefferson 3–34; Martin 3–28; Meggett 3–8; Brisby 2–12.

PASSING

Packers: Favre 27–14–0 (246 yards).

Patriots: Bledsoe 48–25–4 (253 yards).

SCORING	TD	Ru	Pa	Rt	K-PAT	FG	S	PTS
Jacke	0	0	0	0	11/11	5/7	0	26
Bennett	3	3	0	0			0	18
Freeman	3	0	2	1			0	18
Howard	2	0	0	2			0	12
Rison	2	0	2	0			0	12
Favre	1	1	0	0			0	6
Levens	1	0	1	0			0	6
Chmura	0	0	0	0			0	2
TEAM	12	4	5	3	11/11	5/7	0	100
OPPONENTS	6	2	4	0	6/6	2/2	0	48

2-Pt. Conversions: Chmura, TEAM 1–1

PASSING	Att.	Cmp.	Yds.	Cmp%	TD	Int.	Long	Rating
Favre	71	44	617	62.0	5	1	81t	107.5
TEAM	71	44	617	62.0	5	1	81t	107.5
OPPONENTS	126	65	601	51.6	4	9	44	45.8

RUSHING	No.	Yds.	Avg.	Long	TD
Bennett	59	219	3.7	13	3
Levens	39	195	5.0	35	0
Favre	14	35	2.5	23	1
Henderson	4	6	1.5	4	0
McMahon	4	0	0.0	0	0
TEAM	120	455	3.8	35	4
OPPONENTS	45	156	3.5	18t	2

RECEIVING	No.	Yds.	Avg.	Long	TD
Levens	10	156	15.6	66	1
Freeman	9	174	19.3	81t	2
Rison	7	143	20.4	54t	2
Jackson	5	44	8.8	19	0
Bennett	5	23	4.6	10	0
Chmura	3	28	9.3	15	0
Henderson	3	18	6.0	8	0
Beebe	2	31	15.5	29	0
TEAM	44	617	14.0	81t	5
OPPONENTS	65	601	9.2	44	4

INTERCEPTIONS	No.	Yds.	Avg.	Long	TD
Newsome	3	40	13.3	35	0
E. Robinson	2	0	0.0	0	0
B. Williams	1	16	16.0	0	0
Prior	1	8	8.0	8	0
Evans	1	0	0.0	0	0
T. Williams	1	0	0.0	0	0
TEAM	9	64	7.1	35	0
OPPONENTS	1	10	10.0	10	0

PUNTING	No.	Yds.	Avg.	Net	TB	In20	LG	Blk.
Hentrich	15	630	42.0	35.5	2	4	63	0
TEAM	15	630	42.0	35.5	2	4	63	0
OPPONENTS	19	756	39.8	27.7	1	4	53	0

PUNT RETURNS	Ret.	FC	Yds.	Avg.	Long	TD
Howard	9	2	210	23.3	71t	1
Hayes	1	0	0	0.0	0	0
Prior	0	1	0	0.0	0	0
TEAM	10	3	210	21.0	71t	1
OPPONENTS	8	2	57	7.1	20	0

KICKOFF RETURNS	No.	Yds.	Avg.	Long	TD
Howard	9	277	30.8	99t	1
Beebe	1	25	25.0	25	0
TEAM	10	302	30.2	99t	1
OPPONENTS	17	296	17.4	33	0

FIELD GOALS	1-19	20-29	30-39	40-49	50+
Jacke	0/0	1/1	4/4	0/2	0/0
TEAM	0/0	1/1	4/4	0/2	0/0
OPPONENTS	0/0	2/2	0/0	0/0	0/0

No.	Name	Pos.	Ht.	Wt.	Age	College	Hometown
26	Herb Adderley	DB	6-0	200	27	Michigan State	Philadelphia, Pa.
82	Lionel Aldridge	DE	6-4	245	25	Utah State	Evergreen, La.
88	Bill Anderson	TE	6-3	225	30	Tennessee	Hendersonville, N.C.
44	Donny Anderson	HB	6-3	220	23	Texas Tech	Borger, Tex.
57	Ken Bowman	C	6-3	230	24	Wisconsin	Milan, Ill.
12	Zeke Bratkowski	QB	6-3	200	35	Georgia	Danville, Ill.
78	Bob Brown	DE	6-6	265	26	Arkansas AM&N	Bonita, La.
40	Tom Brown	DB	6-1	195	26	Maryland	Reading, Pa.
60	Lee Roy Caffey	LB	6-3	250	25	Texas A&M	Thorndale, Tex.
34	Don Chandler	PK	6-2	210	32	Florida	Tulsa, Okla.
56	Tommy Joe Crutcher	LB	6-3	230	25	Texas Christian	McKinney, Tex.
50	Bill Curry	C	6-2	235	24	Georgia Tech	Atlanta, Ga.
84	Carroll Dale	WR	6-2	200	28	Virginia Tech	Wise, Va.
87	Willie Davis	DE	6-3	245	32	Grambling	Lisbon, La.

No.	Name	Pos.	Ht.	Wt.	Age	College	Hometown
86	Boyd Dowler	WR	6-5	225	29	Colorado	Cheyenne, Wyo.
81	Marv Fleming	TE	6-4	235	24	Utah	Longuien, Tex.
68	Gale Gillingham	G	6-3	250	22	Minnesota	Madison, Wisc.
33	Jim Grabowski	FB	6-2	225	22	Illinois	Chicago, Ill.
75	Forrest Gregg	T	6-4	250	33	Southern Methodist	Birthright, Tex.
43	Doug Hart	DB	6-0	190	27	Arlington State	Handley, Tex.
45	Dave Hathcock	DB	6-0	190	23	Memphis State	Memphis, Tenn.
5	Paul Hornung	HB	6-3	215	31	Notre Dame	Louisville, Ky.
21	Bob Jeter	DB	6-1	205	29	Iowa	Union, S.C.
74	Henry Jordan	DT	6-3	250	31	Virginia	Emporia, Va.
77	Ron Kostelnik	DT	6-2	260	27	Cincinnati	Colver, Pa.
64	Jerry Kramer	G	6-3	245	30	Idaho	Jordan, Mont.
80	Bob Long	WR	6-3	190	25	Wichita State	McKeesport, Pa.
27	Red Mack	WR	5-10	180	29	Notre Dame	Allison Park, Pa.

No.	Name	Pos.	Ht.	Wt.	Age	College	Hometown
85	Max McGee	WR	6-3	205	34	Tulane	Saxton City, Nev.
66	Ray Nitschke	LB	6-3	240	30	Illinois	Elmwood Park, Ill.
22	Elijah Pitts	HB	6-1	205	27	Philander Smith	Conway, Ark.
89	Dave Robinson	LB	6-3	245	25	Penn State	Mt. Holly, N.J.
76	Bob Skoronski	T	6-3	250	32	Indiana	Ansonia, Conn.
15	Bart Starr	QB	6-1	200	32	Alabama	Montgomery, Ala.
31	Jim Taylor	FB	6-0	215	31	Louisiana State	New Orleans, La.
63	Fuzzy Thurston	G	6-1	245	33	Valparaiso	Altoona, Wisc.
37	Phil Vandersea	LB	6-3	225	23	Massachusetts	Whitinsville, Mass.
73	Jim Weatherwax	DT	6-7	275	24	Los Angeles State	Porterville, Calif.
24	Willie Wood	DB	5-10	190	30	Southern California	Washington, D.C.
72	Steve Wright	T	6-6	250	24	Alabama	Louisville, Ky.

No.	Name	Pos.	Ht.	Wt.	Age	College	Hometown
26	Herb Adderley	DB	6-0	200	28	Michigan State	Philadelphia, Pa.
82	Lionel Aldridge	DE	6-4	245	26	Utah State	Evergreen, La.
44	Donny Anderson	HB	6-3	220	24	Texas Tech	Borger, Tex.
57	Ken Bowman	C	6-3	230	25	Wisconsin	Milan, Ill.
12	Zeke Bratkowski	QB	6-3	200	36	Georgia	Danville, Ill.
83	Allen Brown	TE	6-4	230	24	Mississippi	Natchez, Miss.
78	Bob Brown	DE	6-6	265	27	Arkansas AM&N	Bonita, La.
40	Tom Brown	DB	6-1	195	27	Maryland	Reading, Pa.
60	Lee Roy Caffey	LB	6-3	250	26	Texas A&M	Thorndale, Tex.
88	Dick Capp	TE	6-3	235	23	Boston College	Portland, Me.
34	Don Chandler	PK	6-2	210	33	Florida	Tulsa, Okla.
56	Tommy Joe Crutcher	LB	6-3	230	26	Texas Christian	McKinney, Tex.
84	Carroll Dale	WR	6-2	200	29	Virginia Tech	Wise, Va.
87	Willie Davis	DE	6-3	245	33	Grambling	Lisbon, La.
86	Boyd Dowler	WR	6-5	225	30	Colorado	Cheyenne, Wyo.
55	Jim Flanigan	LB	6-3	240	21	Pittsburgh	West Mifflin, Pa.

No.	Name	Pos.	Ht.	Wt.	Age	College	Hometown
81	Marv Fleming	TE	6-4	235	25	Utah	Longuien, Tex.
68	Gale Gillingham	G	6-3	250	23	Minnesota	Madison, Wisc.
33	Jim Grabowski	FB	6-2	225	23	Illinois	Chicago, Ill.
75	Forrest Gregg	T	6-4	250	34	Southern Methodist	Birthright, Tex.
43	Doug Hart	DB	6-0	190	28	Arlington State	Handley, Tex.
13	Don Horn	QB	6-2	195	22	San Diego State	Woodland, Calif.
50	Bob Hyland	C/T	6-5	255	21	Boston College	White Plains, N.Y.
27	Claudis James	WR	6-2	190	21	Jackson State	Colombia, Miss.
21	Bob Jeter	DB	6-1	205	30	Iowa	Union, S.C.
74	Henry Jordan	DT	6-3	250	32	Virginia	Emporia, Va.
77	Ron Kostelnik	DT	6-2	260	28	Cincinnati	Colver, Pa.
64	Jerry Kramer	G	6-3	245	31	Idaho	Jordan, Mont.
80	Bob Long	WR	6-3	190	26	Wichita State	McKeesport, Pa.
85	Max McGee	WR	6-3	205	35	Tulane	Saxton City, Nev.

No.	Name	Pos.	Ht.	Wt.	Age	College	Hometown
30	Chuck Mercein	FB	6-2	225	24	Yale	Milwaukee, Wisc.
66	Ray Nitschke	LB	6-3	240	31	Illinois	Elmwood Park, Ill.
22	Elijah Pitts	HB	6-1	205	28	Philander Smith	Conway, Ark.
89	Dave Robinson	LB	6-3	245	26	Penn State	Mt. Holly, N.J.
45	John Rowser	DB	6-1	180	22	Michigan	Detroit, Mich.
76	Bob Skoronski	T	6-3	250	33	Indiana	Ansonia, Conn.
15	Bart Starr	QB	6-1	200	33	Alabama	Montgomery, Ala.
63	Fuzzy Thurston	G	6-1	245	34	Valparaiso	Altoona, Wisc.
73	Jim Weatherwax	DT	6-7	275	25	Los Angeles State	Porterville, Calif.
23	Travis Williams	HB	6-1	210	21	Arizona State	Phoenix, Ariz.
36	Ben Wilson	FB	6-1	230	27	Southern California	Houston, Tex.
24	Willie Wood	DB	5-10	190	31	Southern California	Washington, D.C.
72	Steve Wright	T	6-6	250	25	Alabama	Louisville, Ky.

SUNDAY, JANUARY 15, 1967

| Kansas City | 0 | 10 | 0 | 0—10 |
| Green Bay | 7 | 7 | 14 | 7—35 |

SCORING

FIRST QUARTER

GB   M. McGee 37 yd. pass from B. Starr (D. Chandler, kick)

SECOND QUARTER

KC   C. McClinton 7 yd. pass from L. Dawson (M. Mercer, kick)

GB   J. Taylor 14 yd. run (D. Chandler, kick)

KC   M. Mercer 31 yd. Field Goal

THIRD QUARTER

GB   E. Pitts 5 yd. run (D. Chandler, kick)

GB   M. McGee 13 yd. pass from B. Starr (D. Chandler, kick)

FOURTH QUARTER

GB   E. Pitts 1 yd. run (D. Chandler, kick)

TEAM STATISTICS

	Packers	**Chiefs**
First Downs	21	17
Total Net Yards	358	239
Total Plays	64	64
Net Yards Rushing	130	72
Net Yards Passing	228	167
Passes (A-C-I)	24–16–1	33–17–1
Penalties-Yards	4–40	4–26
Fumbles (No.-Lost)	1–0	1–0

RUSHING

Packers: Taylor 16–53; Pitts 11–45; Anderson 4–0; Grabowski 2–2.

Chiefs: Garrett 6–17; McClinton 6–16; Dawson 3–24; Coan 3–1; Beathard 1–14.

RECEIVING

Packers: McGee 7–138; Dale 4–59; Fleming 2–22; Pitts 2–32; Taylor 1–(–1).

Chiefs: Buford 4–67; Taylor 4–57; Garrett 3–28; McClinton 2–34; Arbanas 2–30; Carolan 1–7; Coan 1–5.

PASSING

Packers: Starr 23–16–1 (250 yards); Bratkowski 1–0–0.

Chiefs: Dawson 27–16–1 (211 yards); Beathard 5–1–0 (17 yards).

SUNDAY, DECEMBER 31, 1967

Dallas	0	10	0	7—17
Green Bay	7	7	0	7—21

SCORING

FIRST QUARTER

GB   B. Dowler 8 yd. pass from B. Starr (D. Chandler, kick)

SECOND QUARTER

GB   B. Dowler 46 yd. pass from B. Starr (D. Chandler, kick)

DC   G. Andrie returned fumble 7 yds. (D. Villanueva, kick)

DC   D. Villanueva 21 yd. Field Goal

FOURTH QUARTER

DC   L. Rentzel 50 yd. pass from D. Reeves (D. Villanueva, kick)

GB   B. Starr 1 yd. run (D. Chandler, kick)

TEAM STATISTICS

	Packers	Cowboys
First Downs	18	11
Total Net Yards	195	192
Total Plays	64	60
Net Yards Rushing	80	92
Net Yards Passing	115	100
Passes (A-C-I)	24–14–0	26–11–1
Penalties-Yards	2–10	7–58
Fumbles (No.-Lost)	3–2	3–1

RUSHING

Packers: Anderson 18–35; Mercein 6–20; Williams 4–13; Wilson 3–11; Starr 1–1.

Cowboys: Perkins 17–51; Reeves 13–42; Meredith 1–9; Baynham 1–(–2); Clarke 1–(–8).

RECEIVING

Packers: Dowler 4–77; Anderson 4–44; Dale 3–44; Mercein 2–22; Williams 1–4.

Cowboys: Hayes 3–16; Reeves 3–11; Rentzel 2–61; Clarke 2–24; Baynham 1–3.

PASSING

Packers: Starr 24–14–0 (191 yards).

Cowboys: Meredith 25–10–1 (59 yards); Reeves 1–1–0 (50 yards).

SUNDAY, JANUARY 14, 1968

Oakland	0	7	0	7—14
Green Bay	3	13	10	7—33

SCORING

FIRST QUARTER

GB   D. Chandler 39 yd. Field Goal

SECOND QUARTER

GB   D. Chandler 20 yd. Field Goal

GB   B. Dowler 62 yd. pass from B. Starr (D. Chandler, kick)

OK   Miller 23 yd. pass from D. Lamonica (G. Blanda, kick)

GB   D. Chandler 43 yd. Field Goal

THIRD QUARTER

GB   D. Anderson 2 yd. run (D. Chandler, kick)

GB   D. Chandler 31 yd. Field Goal

FOURTH QUARTER

GB   H. Adderley 60 yd. interception return (D. Chandler, kick)

OK   Miller 23 yd. pass from D. Lamonica (G. Blanda, kick)

TEAM STATISTICS

	Packers	Raiders
First Downs	19	16
Total Net Yards	325	291
Total Plays	69	57
Net Yards Rushing	163	105
Net Yards Passing	162	186
Passes (A-C-I)	24–13–0	34–15–1
Penalties-Yards	1–12	4–31
Fumbles (No.-Lost)	0–0	3–2

RUSHING

Packers: Wilson 17–65; Anderson 14–48; Williams 8–36; Starr 1–14; Mercein 1–0.

Raiders: Dixon 12–52; Todd 2–37; Banaszak 6–16.

RECEIVING

Packers: Dale 4–43; Fleming 4–35; Anderson 2–18; Dowler 2–71; McGee 1–35.

Raiders: Miller 5–84; Biletnikoff 2–10; Banaszak 4–69; Cannon 2–25; Dixon 1–3; Wells 1–17.

PASSING

Packers: Starr 13–24–0; Bratkowski 0–0–0.

Raiders: Lamonica 15–34–1.

Acknowledgments

If *Distant Replay*, the story of a reunion of Vince Lombardi's Packers, was the son of *Instant Replay*, the diary of a season with Vince Lombardi's Packers, then this book is the grandson. The three put together are, in several ways, a family chronicle.

I wrote the first two in collaboration with Jerry Kramer, and I must acknowledge his contributions to this volume. Jerry offered his encouragement, his observations, his thoughts, and his second of four sons. His son Dan, a gifted photographer who recently circled the globe with his camera, emulating a trip Mark Twain had survived a century earlier, took the sixteen pages of pictures that appear inside this book.

The cover photographs of Lombardi and Bart Starr and Mike Holmgren and Brett Favre were taken by Vernon Biever, who also took the cover photo for *Instant*

Replay, a magnificent portrait of a mud-caked Jerry Kramer. Vernon Biever's son Jim is also in the family business, which is capturing on film the spirit and substance of the Green Bay Packers. The photo inside the back cover, of Favre and me, was taken by Dave Thomason, the founder of the Official Brett Favre Fan Club, a private pilot who often flies Favre around the country.

I appreciate the work of the Kramer dynasty, but the one individual who put the greatest time and energy and thought into helping me on this project was Jim Nagy. Fresh out of the University of Michigan, Jim had the good sense to serve an internship in the Packers' public relations office for seven months, starting with training camp 1996 and ending with Super Bowl XXXI. And I had the good sense to have Jim spend the next seven weeks gathering, assessing, and organizing material that would enable me to write this book. He made my task immensely easier and considerably more pleasant.

I want to thank Lee Remmel, the Packers' executive director of public relations, for allowing me to steal Jim Nagy from him and borrow histories of the team, and for the great cooperation and assistance I got from his associates, Jeff Blumb, Mark Schiefelbein, Paula Martin, and Aaron Popkey. Bob Harlan, Ron Wolf, and especially Mike Holmgren all took time from their busy schedules to talk to me. So did most of the assistant coaches and almost all of the present Packer players and many of the old. Thanks, too, to Sue Kluck, Mike Holmgren's secretary, for setting up my meetings with the coach, and to Linda McCrossin, who guards the public relations wing, for the cookies and kind greetings.

The Brown County Library's Mary Jane Herber, who was related by marriage to the Packers' Hall of Fame quarterback, Arnie Herber—it's a small world, the Packer world—was an invaluable guide to the lore and history of the area, and Rachael Berman, too, unearthed a wealth of background information.

My daughter Joanna and Andrew Kasdan transcribed tapes for me, and my son Jeremy occasionally took time from his ESPN chores and his social schedule to check out a football, or literary, reference. Dan Cohen, a computer wizard who works at the Classic Sports Network, saved me from mechanical disaster countless times. And Joe Valerio, the producer of *The Sports Reporters*, the weekly show I host on ESPN, and Doug Warshaw, my friend and former producer, now senior vice-president at Classic Sports Network, read drafts of this work and provided informed counsel.

Once again, as I did in my previous book and will do in my next, I would like to thank David Black, my literary agent, and Lou Aronica, publisher at Avon Books, for setting up this venture and nurturing it. They both shared my faith in the 1996 Green Bay Packers; they are too young to have shared my faith in the 1966 Packers.

And, finally, thanks to Trish McLeod, my beautiful wife, on the brink of her big birthday, for putting up with me.